My Tax Tutor

For
Small Business
Owners

What every small business owner should know about their taxes.

By Joni M. Becker, CPA

Copyrighted January, 2012

ISBN # 978-1469943039

First Printing, 2009

Second Printing, 2012

Printed in the United States of America

Cover Photo Image: David Castillo Dominici / FreeDigitalPhotos.net

Legal Stuff

While every effort has been made to be as accurate as possible, tax law is a fluid thing. I cannot be responsible for errors made by relying on the information in this publication. Also, each individual tax return is complicated and made up of various interrelated parts, because of this I cannot be responsible for errors made by your not contacting a tax professional to help you assess your whole situation.

The purpose of this book is to inform you about our tax system and to serve as a beginning point of a conversation with your own tax professional. It is not meant to be relied on as legal authority or accounting advice in preparing your individual return(s), business or personal.

About the Author

Joni M. Becker, CPA –

Mrs. Becker has a Master's Degree in Business Taxation from the University of Minnesota, received in 1992. She is a QuickBooks Certified ProAdvisor and a member of the Minnesota Society of CPA's.

Joni spent 5 years teaching accounting and tax classes at two East Tennessee colleges and one year at St. John's University in Collegeville, Minnesota. It is from her love of teaching that My Tax Tutor was born.

Joni has been helping small businesses, ranging from small mom and pop operations to multi-million dollar corporations, save taxes for over 18 years. She is currently employed at a public accounting firm, D.C. Schluter, Ltd. in south central Minnesota.

"I am committed to helping small and home-based businesses of all kinds arrange their affairs so they *pay the least amount of tax legally possible.*"

Joni has been married to husband Dale for over 26 years, and they live with 1 dog and 3 cats in Faribault, Minnesota.

She can be contacted at:

D.C. Schluter, Ltd.
1225 Highway 60 West
Faribault, MN 55021
E-Mail: joni@MyTaxTutor.com

My Tax Tutor

For
Small Business
Owners

What every small business owner should know about their taxes.

Table of Contents

Business versus Hobby And Why Should I Care?

You may not have even thought of this, but whether your activities qualify as a business or as a hobby is a very important distinction. If the IRS determines that your activities are a hobby (**no matter what you say it is**), the amount that can be written off as expenses is <u>very</u> limited and you are not allowed to show a loss at all! Worse than that, even, is <u>any and all income</u> from a hobby <u>must be included in taxable income</u>!

The thing to remember here is it is not what you think your activities are – IT IS WHAT THE IRS THINKS THAT COUNTS.

Because of this, it is very important that you set your activities up in the beginning to be a legitimate business with no chance that the IRS could come back and determine that it was a hobby instead. This is especially true if you are starting a business part-time while you maintain your regular job.

This is best shown through an example:

HOBBY:

Let's say that I have $40,000 of income that includes $38,000 of wages from my full-time job and $2,000 of income from my hobby.

I have $10,000 of expenses associated with my hobby including $1,000 of home mortgage interest and real estate taxes for my home office that I would be able to deduct as Itemized Deductions on Schedule A of Form 1040 with or without a business.

So I include my $38,000 of wages and $2,000 of hobby income on the front of my Form 1040. Then I go to my Schedule A and deduct the $1,000 of interest and taxes on the appropriate lines. Of the remaining $9,000 of expenses, I can only deduct another $1,000! Hobby expenses are only deductible up to the amount of hobby income. $2,000 of income less $1,000 of interest and taxes, leaves $1,000 of deductible hobby expenses.

But it gets worse. The additional $1,000 of expenses are deducted as Miscellaneous Expenses subject to a 2% floor! This means that of the remaining $1,000 of expenses that I am allowed to deduct, I can actually only deduct $200! First I calculate the 2% floor as $40,000 income ($38,000 wages + $2,000 hobby income) x 2% = $800 – this is the non-deductible amount. Then I calculate the deductible amount as $1,000 - $800 = $200.

But it gets even worse! I would only take the Itemized Deductions on Schedule A if the total of all of my itemized deductions was more than the Standard Deduction allowed by the IRS. The amount of your standard deduction depends on your filing status, such as single, married filing joint, head of household, etc. and changes every year.

Best Case Scenario: I include the $2,000 of hobby income on my tax return. I can deduct $1,000 of mortgage interest and property taxes (that I would be able to deduct anyway) and an additional $200 as Miscellaneous Itemized Deductions subject to the 2% floor. The other $8,800 of expenses are lost to me.

Worst Case Scenario: I include the $2,000 of hobby income on my tax return. Because I don't qualify to take Itemized Deductions, <u>I cannot take any of the $10,000 of expenses</u> associated with my hobby!

BUSINESS:

Now, let's look at the same scenario with a legitimate small business.

I have the same $38,000 in wages from my regular job, but now I have set up my activities to make sure they qualify as a small business. I have the same $2,000 in income and the same $10,000 in expenses.

If I am a sole proprietor (single person business) I will file a Schedule C, Profit and Loss from a Business, along with my Form 1040 at the end of the year.

I will report $2,000 in income on my Schedule C and will be able to claim ALL $10,000 of business expenses.

This leaves me with an $8,000 loss from my business that I can use to reduce my wage income to only $30,000! A big difference from the hobby scenario, isn't it? Remember, with the hobby scenario, I had $40,000 of income and only $1,200 in allowed expenses in the best case!

How can you make sure your activities will be seen as a business by the IRS?

Basically, the IRS takes the position that if it looks like a duck and walks like a duck and quacks like a duck, it must be a duck. You want to make sure that your activities look like a business and are conducted like a business.

You especially want to give the appearance that your activities are conducted with the intent to make a profit. You don't <u>have</u> to make a profit, you just have to show that you <u>intend</u> to make a profit!

To determine whether the activity was conducted with the intent to earn a profit, the IRS will look at the following factors:

1. **Whether the activity is conducted like a business.**
   Do you have a separate checking account for this activity?
   Are you keeping good records?
   What type of marketing and promotional efforts are being engaged in?
   What type of attempts are being made to avoid or eliminate losses?

2. **The expertise of the taxpayer.**
   What was your reason for engaging in this activity?
   Do you have any previous experience in this or a similar type of activity?
   What types of preparations did you make prior to engaging in this activity (training, classes)?
   Are you following accepted business practices?

3. **The time and effort expended.**
   What is the amount of time and effort expended in running this activity?
   Do you have assistance from others?

4. **Previous success of the taxpayer in similar activities.**

14

Has the taxpayer had success in a related or similar activities?

5. **Income and loss history from the activity.**
How many years has the activity reported losses? Has the activity had a history of up and down years?

6. **Relationship of income to losses in the activity.**
Has the activity ever had a profit? What is the size of the profits versus the losses?

7. **Financial status of the taxpayer.**
Is there income from another source to support the taxpayer?
Does the activity have the appearance of a possible tax shelter?

8. **Elements of personal recreation in the activity.**
Does the activity lend itself more to personal recreation than to business purposes?
Especially scrutinized are business involving gardening activities or pleasure boat rentals.

9. **Expectation of increase in asset value.**
Can the taxpayer reasonably expect the assets of the activity to increase in value over time?
If asset values are expected to increase, this fact can take the place of a profit motive.

There is no exact right or wrong answer to these questions. The answers to all of the questions are taken as a whole to determine a business versus a hobby. Every case is judged on its own facts and circumstances.

Tax law includes a provision that states if an activity shows a profit for three out of the previous five years, the activity is automatically considered as engaged in for profit. At that point, the burden of proof is shifted to the IRS and it is up to them to prove that it is a hobby.

Does that mean if your business does not show a profit in three out of five years it will automatically be considered a hobby? No. Again, it goes back to facts and circumstances in each case. I had a business that showed a loss for 10 years and I was never questioned on it by the IRS. But, I conducted it as a business and kept good records (which we will discuss next).

By knowing what the IRS is looking for, you can be prepared to defend your activities as a legitimate business. Be very careful to set up and conduct your activities as a business and you will have no problems with the IRS.

Starting Your Business and Keeping Records

Whether you are new to owning your own business or a seasoned pro, this chapter is packed full of great information and well worth a read.

Forms of Business

The first decision you have to make is what form of business you will use for your new venture. There are pros and cons for each form and there are legal and tax consequences of each choice. I will just talk about the tax implications here, but you should seek competent legal advice as well as speaking to your tax professional before you make a final decision.

Sole proprietorships are probably the most common form used for small businesses. A sole proprietorship is simply one individual starting a business with no formal legal form. It is the simplest form to start and maintain. You would file a Schedule C with your Form 1040 at the end of the year. A sole proprietorship does not offer any liability protection, so all your assets, business and personal, are exposed to lawsuits and other legal actions. You are, also, personally liable for all your business debts.

Partnerships are similar to sole proprietorships except there is more than one person involved. Each person puts money, property, labor or skill, into the business and expects to share in the profits or losses of the business.

Partnerships are what is called a "pass-through" business. They file a tax return, Form 1065, that reports all the income, expenses, gains and losses of the business, but they do not pay tax. Instead, the results of operations is 'passed through' to the individual partners. The partners then report his or her share, and pays taxes on those amounts, on their own Form 1040 return.

Corporations are their own legal entities. In other words, owners can come and go, but the business can go on indefinitely. In forming a corporation, prospective shareholders exchange money, property, or some combination of both, for stock in the corporation.

A corporation, generally, takes the same deductions as a sole proprietorship or partnership, but they file, Form 1120, and pay their own taxes. The profits of the corporation are then, also, taxed to the shareholders as they are passed out as dividends. This is the dreaded 'double taxation' that you may have heard others talking about.

S Corporations can be used to avoid double taxation. A corporation must meet certain criteria to be eligible to elect S status, but most small, domestic corporations qualify. An S corporation is another "pass-through" form of business. They file a tax return, Form1120S, but the income, expense, gains and losses, 'pass through' and are reported on the shareholders' individual returns.

Limited Liability Companies are becoming more and more popular. Limited liability companies are formed under state laws and, as such, are disregarded by the IRS for tax purposes. When setting up a limited liability company, the owners can chose (elect) to have it treated, for federal tax purposes, as a partnership, a corporation, or an entity disregarded as an entity separate from its owner (a sole proprietorship). Which tax return a limited liability company files, depends on how they chose to be treated when they are set up.

The advantages of an LLC (limited liability company) include the ease of set up and maintenance (easier than a corporation) and the fact that the members of the LLC cannot be held liable (be made to pay) for the company's debts.

Federal Identification Numbers

You have to have a federal identification number in order to file a tax return and correspond with the IRS. Most of us already have one federal identification number, our social security number. If you are a sole proprietor and do not have any employees, you can use your social security number as your federal identification number for your business.

If you use any other form of business, or have employees, you will need to apply for and obtain an Employer Identification Number (EIN) using form SS-4. You can apply on line and receive your number immediately by going to www.IRS.gov.

Tax Years

The next decision you need to make is the tax year that you will use. For most of us, this is easy. We simply use a calendar year, January 1 through December 31, as we do for our other tax returns. You are required to use a calendar year if you keep no books, have no annual accounting period or are required to use one by the IRS.

There is an option of using a fiscal tax year other than a calendar year. A fiscal year can be made up of any 12 consecutive months ending on the last day of any month except December. Regular, or 'C', corporations may choose to use a fiscal year instead of a tax year, but for the majority of us, it is just easier to use the calendar year.

Once you have chosen a tax year, which you do by filing your first tax return, you must get permission from the IRS to change it.

Accounting Methods

Your accounting method is a set of rules that determines when and how income and expenses are reported. You chose this method, again, when you file your first tax return. There are two basic accounting methods:

1. Cash Method is used to report income in the tax year it is <u>received</u> and expenses are deducted in the year they are <u>paid</u>.
2. Accrual Method is used to report income in the tax year it is <u>earned</u> and expenses are deducted in the year they are <u>incurred</u>.

For example, you complete a job in December and send a bill to your client. They pay you in January. If you are a cash basis taxpayer, the income will be reported in January, when the cash is received. If you are an accrual basis taxpayer, the income will be reported in December when it is earned.

On the other side, you receive and pay your December electric bill in January. If you are a cash basis taxpayer, you will report the expense in January, when the cash is paid. If you are an accrual basis taxpayer, you will report the expense in December, when the expense was incurred.

Once established, if you want to change your accounting method, you must get permission from the IRS.

Let me pause here for just one second and talk about the difference between cash and income. I get a lot of my clients asking, "How can I have income, I have no money?" The simple answer is that cash and income are two different things. Remember that income is measured as Revenue (Sales) minus Expenses. You can spend your cash on lots of things that don't affect your income such as purchasing a piece of equipment or paying down debt. These transactions use your cash, but don't affect your net income.

Business Taxes

The form of business you use is going to determine what kind of taxes you have to pay. There are four basic kinds of federal taxes that a business owner may come across: income tax, self-employment tax, employment taxes, and excise taxes.

Income tax is primarily what this book deals with although we may lightly touch on self-employment and employment taxes. Each business must file some sort of income tax form each year, even if it is just an information return like a partnership files.

The federal tax system is a pay-as-you-go system, meaning that in a perfect world you would have the exact amount you owe paid in at the end of the year. For employees, this is accomplished through the withholding system and taxes are deducted from each paycheck. For us small business owners, though, we must rely on using estimated taxes.

Estimated taxes are due four times a year, April 15, June 15, September 15 and January 15 of the following year. Payments are supposed to be in four equal installments. If they are not, you will be penalized even if you have the total amount paid.

Let's say your taxes are estimated for the next year to be $10,000. The IRS wants to receive $2,500 four times a year from you. But let's say, business is slow at the beginning of the year and you don't pay anything on April 15, but make it up on June 15 by paying $5,000. Guess what? You will be penalized based on the $2,500 from April 15 through June 15, when the IRS actually received the money. So, even if you pay all you owe, you may still be liable for a penalty. I know, it's not fair, it's just the IRS way of doing things.

There is a safe harbor rule with estimated taxes. If you pay in 100% of the tax you owed for the prior year, you will not be penalized even if your tax liability is considerably higher this year. That is assuming that you pay one fourth of the amount on each of the due dates, of course.

Self-employment taxes are the equivalent of an employee's Social Security and Medicare payments. A W-2 employee pays (as a deduction on their paycheck) one half of these taxes and the employer pays the other half. When we work for ourselves, we get to pay both the employer's and the employee's share of our own Social Security and Medicare. Self-employment tax is, basically, 15.3% of your net income as a business owner unless you have a corporation (C or S) and pay yourself with a paycheck. You do get to deduct one-half of your self-employment tax on page one of your 1040. (The rate for self-employment taxes for 2011 and the first 60 days of

22

2012 is 13.3% due to a reduction in the Social Security rate. Congress may or may not extend this past the first 60 days of 2012.)

If you have employees, you will be responsible for deducting Federal Withholding, Social Security and Medicare from your employees' paychecks. Then, you need to add the employer share of Social Security and Medicare to what you withheld from the employees and pay the money over to the IRS.   For the majority of small businesses, this payment is due by the 15th of the following month and is deposited in a local bank or paid over the internet using the IRS's EFTPS system.

Most states also have mandatory withholding for employees in their states. Check with your tax professional for your state requirements.

You will also be responsible for Unemployment taxes, Federal and usually state also. For Federal Unemployment, you pay tax only on the first $7,000 of an employees wages. Once that threshold is met, you don't pay anymore until next year. If you pay all of your state unemployment on time, then the federal rate is 0.8%. If you have not paid all your state unemployment in a timely manner, the federal rate goes to 6.2%! A big difference.

Now, I hear some of you saying, "Well, I'll just pay everyone as an independent contractor and not have to worry about employment taxes." Whoa, hold on. The IRS has very definite rules about who is an employee and who is an independent contractor. This is the subject of a later chapter, but let me say here that if you pay everyone as an independent contractor and the IRS later determines that they were actually employees, you not only get to pay penalties and interest on all the taxes that should have been paid, but you also have to pay the employees' share of taxes that should have been deducted in the first place. This can be a very expensive mistake; one you don't want to make.

Federal excise taxes are rare for most of us small business owners, but I do want to mention them here. You may owe excise taxes if you manufacture or sell certain products, operate certain kinds of businesses, use various kinds of equipment, facilities or products, or receive payments for certain services. Kind of vague, isn't it.

Excise taxes mainly involve environmental taxes, communications and air transportation taxes, fuel taxes, tax on the first retail sale of heavy trucks, trailers and tractors, or manufacturing taxes on the sale or use of a variety of different articles. Most of us don't have to worry about it, but you need to check with your tax professional to make sure you don't owe any of these taxes.

You also need to check with your tax professional regarding your liability on state taxes.

Recordkeeping

The need to keep good, accurate records is not just to make sure you file an accurate tax return, it will also help you run your business. Without good financial records how can you monitor the progress of your business, prepare financial statements, identify where your money is coming from and where it is going, or defend yourself in case of an audit? In other words, it is very hard to run a successful business without keeping good records.

There are so many inexpensive recordkeeping softwares today that you really have no excuse not to keep good business records. The largest majority of my clients use QuickBooks, but if you're just starting out you may want to look into Quicken or Money. QuickBooks has a program called Simple Start that is free and you can easily upgrade to QuickBooks as your business grows. You can find Simple Start at www.QuickBooks.com

For the most part, the law does not require any specific kind of recordkeeping system. You can choose any system as long as it clearly shows your income and expenses. The business that you are in may determine the type of records you need to keep for federal tax purposes.

If you have more than one business, you also want to make sure that you keep complete and separate records for each business. You also want to make sure that you keep your business records separate from your personal records. By all means, the first thing you should do is set up a separate bank account for your business so those records are kept separate from your personal records and there is no co-mingling of funds.

Your recordkeeping system should include a summary of your business transactions. They must show your gross income, as well as deductions and credits. This is primarily done through your checking account, thus the need for a separate business account.

You will also need supporting documents for transactions. These may include sales slips, paid bills, invoices, receipts, deposit slips and cancelled checks. It is important to keep these documents because they support the entries in your books and on your tax return. Keep them in an orderly fashion and in a safe place.

Gross receipts are the income you receive from your business. The documentation that you would need to support these amounts may be cash register tapes, bank deposit slips, receipt books, invoices, credit card charge slips and forms 1099-Misc.

For purchases that your business makes, documents to keep are canceled checks, cash register tape receipts, credit card receipts and bills from your vendors.

There are special documentation rules for travel, transportation, entertainment and gift expenses. I will talk about this more in the specific deduction section, but let me mention here that the main thing is to write on the receipt who you were meeting with, the business purpose for the meeting and the date and time.

If you are purchasing assets (equipment, machinery, furniture, etc.) for your business, you must keep detailed records as you will be depreciating these items instead of expensing them. More on that later, but to begin you will need to track when and how you acquired the asset, purchase price, cost of any improvements, any Section 179 taken, prior deductions for depreciation, how you use the asset, when and how you got rid of the asset, selling price and expenses of the sale. You will want to keep all of these records for as long as you own the asset, and then some.

You must keep your records for 'as long as they may be needed for the administration of any provision of the Internal Revenue Code.' Scary. Basically, this means you must keep them as long as the statute of limitations on a particular return is in effect.

For most of us, the statute of limitations is 3 years from the filing date of the return, including extensions. If you have underreported your income by more than 25% of the income shown on the return, the statute of limitations extends to 6 years. If you file a claim for a loss from worthless securities or a bad debt deduction, the statute of limitations is 7 years.

If you file a fraudulent return, though, there is no statute of limitations. So, you need to use your best judgment on this. I usually keep my records for 7 years and then burn or shred them.

NOTE: Do you want to audit proof your taxes? Then you must keep excellent records. If your records clearly support the amounts reported on your tax return, then there will be no need for an adjustment by the IRS in case you are called in for an audit. I cannot stress the importance of good recordkeeping enough.

So, What Can I Deduct?

As a CPA, serving primarily small business clients, the most common question I am asked is, "What can I deduct?" and I think, "Where do I start?"

In order for your business expenses to be deductible, they must fall within certain guidelines; guidelines that can, at times, be somewhat vague. First and foremost, the expenses **must be incurred due to your trade, business or profession**. Personal expenses are generally not deductible except for a very few specifically allowed by Congress such as home mortgage interest and property taxes.

To qualify as a "trade", "business" or "profession" your activities must be carried out regularly and with an _honest attempt_ to make a profit. Carried on regularly does not mean every day, but on a regular basis. You may have a roadside vegetable stand that is only open 4 months out of the year, but it is open every year, so it is carried on regularly.

And an honest attempt to make a profit does not mean that you **have** to make a profit for your expenses to be deductible. You just have to working towards making a profit. Basically, what the IRS is saying here is that you have to be running your business as a business in order for the expenses to qualify for deduction.

Secondly, your business expenses must be **ordinary, necessary and reasonable**. Ordinary expenses are those that are common and accepted for your type of business. Necessary expenses qualify for deduction if they are appropriate and helpful in promoting, developing and maintaining your business.

Keep in mind that the IRS's definition of necessary is somewhat different than what you may normally think of as necessary. Most people think of necessary as something that they can't do without but the IRS gives a very broad meaning to the word. You may be able to run your business without gold embossed stationery, but it may be helpful in promoting your business, so you can deduct it.

The amount that is considered reasonable depends on the facts and circumstances. What is a reasonable amount for one business may not be a reasonable amount for another. Spending $1,000 on gold embossed stationery may be a reasonable amount for a business grossing hundreds of thousands of dollars a year, but may be an unreasonable amount for a business grossing $500 a year. Use your common sense here, if you think it is unreasonable, it probably is. When debating to deduct or not to deduct, I always like to put myself in the IRS's shoes. If I think I can make a good, believable argument for the deduction, I deduct.

Deductions that are likely to invite a second look by the IRS include large travel and entertainment deductions, expenses not typically associated with your type of business, deductions for items of a personal or recreational nature, or deductions that are out of line with the amount of income you're reporting.

As one of my mentors always said, *"When it comes to the IRS, you always want to be a pig, but never a hog because pigs get bred and have more pigs. Hogs get slaughtered."* So be sure to take every legitimate deduction you are entitled to, but don't cross over the line and take ones to which you are not entitled.

Small business owners overpay their taxes by billions of dollars each year because they don't know exactly what they can, or can't, deduct. Don't be one of them.

Remember that each tax deduction you find is like giving yourself a raise.

Next you will find the Small Business Deduction Checklist. Print it out and take a copy of it to your next meeting with your tax professional. It is a good reference point to use to get a conversation started.

Following the checklist will be the A,B,C's of small business tax deductions. This is the meat and potatoes of this book. It is here that you will find the tips, tricks and strategies that will help you keep your hard earned money in your own pocket. The deductions are in alphabetically order for ease of use. Refer back to them often and remember, the best tax planning is done BEFORE a transaction is completed and BEFORE year end.

Small Business Deduction Checklist

All expenses must meet the 4 basic guidelines in order to be deductible:

1. Incurred in connection with your trade, business or profession;
2. Ordinary – common & accepted in your type of business;
3. Necessary – appropriate & helpful in running your business;
4. Reasonable – not lavish or extravagant.

If the deduction is limited by other factors, this is noted next to the deduction. If there are no limits, other than the four listed above, there is will be nothing listed.

Some business expenses must be written off over a period of time instead of in the year purchased. Generally these are business assets that will last more than one year, such as furniture, machinery, equipment and buildings. They are called 'Fixed Assets' or 'Capital Assets'. The process we use to expense these items is called Depreciation. For intangible (non-physical) assets, the process is called Amortization and Depletion for natural resources. Expenses that may qualify for depreciation are noted as such.

The timing of the deduction depends on whether you are a cash basis taxpayer or an accrual basis taxpayer. Generally you choose which one you want to be when you file the first return for your business. Check out Chapter 2 for more information.

Cash basis taxpayers report income when they receive payment (cash in) and deduct expenses when they make the payment (cash out). Accrual basis taxpayers report income when it is earned, no matter when it is received, and deduct expenses when they are incurred, regardless of when they are paid.

For example: Let's say you are a calendar year taxpayer and you receive your December electric bill on January 6th and pay it on January 15th. A cash basis taxpayer would deduct the expense in January, when it is paid. An accrual basis taxpayer would deduct the expense in December, when the expense was incurred.

Deduction	**Limits**
❏ Accounting Fees	May be limited
❏ Advertising	
❏ Air Fare	Limited
❏ Alarms	Fees expensed; System depreciated
❏ Allowance for Bad Debts	Accrual based accounting only
❏ Amortization	Intangibles written off over life of asset
❏ Answering Service	
❏ Antiques	Very Limited
❏ Appraisal Fees	Depends on Type
❏ Assessments-Repairs	
❏ Assessments-Improvements	Not deductible
❏ Association Memberships	Limited by type of association
❏ Athletic Club Memberships	Not deductible
❏ Attorney Fees	
❏ Audits	Limited by type
❏ Automobile Expenses	Limited
❏ Bad Checks	If included in income

❑	Bad Debts	If included in income
❑	Bail Bond Fees	Limited
❑	Bank Charges	
❑	Bankruptcy-Business Only	
❑	Batteries	
❑	Benefits-Employee	Limited
❑	Billboards	
❑	Bonus - Employee	
❑	Bookkeeping Service	
❑	Books	Business related
❑	Bribes	Not deductible if illegal
❑	Broker's Fees	May be limited
❑	Buildings	Depreciated
❑	Business Cards	
❑	Business Gifts	Up to $25 each
❑	Business Licenses	
❑	Campaign Contributions	Not deductible
❑	Cancellation Penalties	
❑	Capital Assets	Depreciated
❑	Carrying Charges	
❑	Cartons	May be part of inventory costs
❑	Casualty Losses	Limited
❑	Catalogs	Expensed or Amortized
❑	Charitable Contributions	Very Limited
❑	Child Care	Limited
❑	Child on Payroll	Limited
❑	Cleaning Service - Premises	
❑	Cleaning Service - Clothing	Limited
❑	Closing Costs	Depends on type

❏	Clothing - Work	Limited
❏	Club Memberships	Depends on type
❏	Coffee Service	
❏	Collection Costs	
❏	Commissions	Depends on type
❏	Commuting	Not Deductible
❏	Compensation - Employee	May be limited
❏	Computers	Depreciated
❏	Conferences	
❏	Consignment	Not deductible until sold
❏	Consultants	
❏	Contests	
❏	Contractors	Depends on type of work
❏	Conventions	May be limited
❏	Copyrights	Amortized
❏	Cost of Goods Sold	
❏	Costumes	
❏	Coupons	
❏	Courier Service	
❏	Credit Cards	Business related
❏	Customs Fees	
❏	Decorating	
❏	Delivery Charges	
❏	Depletion	Depreciation on Natural Resources
❏	Deposits	Limited
❏	Depreciation	Assets expensed over their life
❏	Design Costs	Expensed or Depreciated
❏	Director's Fees	
❏	Discounts	Reduce Income
❏	Displays	Depends on type
❏	Dividends - Corporate	Not deductible
❏	Draws	Not deductible

❑	Driveways	Expensed or Depreciated
❑	Dues	Depends on type
❑	Duties	
❑	Education	May be limited
❑	Electricity	Limited for Home-Based Businesses
❑	Employee Benefits	
❑	Employee Reimbursements	Depends on Type
❑	Employment Agencies	
❑	Entertainment	Limited
❑	Equipment	Depreciated
❑	Estimated Tax Payments	Not deductible
❑	Excise Taxes	
❑	Expense Accounts	Depends on type
❑	Exporting Fees	
❑	Exterminating Service	
❑	Fidelity Bond	
❑	Finders Fees	
❑	Fines	Not deductible if for breaking the law
❑	Fire Protection System	Fees expensed; System depreciated
❑	First Aid Supplies	
❑	Fixed Assets	Depreciated
❑	Fixtures	Depreciated
❑	Flowers	
❑	Food	Limited
❑	Forfeitures	Such as Deposits, Advance Payments
❑	Franchise Fees	Expensed or Amortized
❑	Franchise Taxes	
❑	Freelancers	
❑	Free Samples	

❑	Freight	
❑	Fringe Benefits - Employee	Limited
❑	Finance Charges	
❑	Fuel	May be limited
❑	Furniture	Depreciated
❑	Garbage Service	
❑	Gardening Expense	Not for Home-based Businesses
❑	Gifts - Business	Up to $25 each
❑	Goodwill	Amortized if purchased
❑	Graphic Design	Expensed or Amortized
❑	Greeting Cards	
❑	Gross Receipts Tax	
❑	Guaranteed Payments to Partners	
❑	Guard Dog	
❑	Hobby Losses	Not Deductible
❑	Home Demonstrations	
❑	Home Office	Very Limited
❑	Housing Allowance - Employees	Limited
❑	Illegal Expenses	Not deductible
❑	Importing Costs	May be part of inventory costs
❑	Improvements	Depreciated
❑	Income Taxes	Depends on type
❑	Incorporation Fees	Amortized
❑	Independent Contractors	
❑	Insurance - Automobile	May be limited
❑	Insurance - Disability	Employees only
❑	Insurance - Errors & Omissions	
❑	Insurance - Health	May be limited

❑	Insurance - Liability	
❑	Insurance - Life	Employees only; limited
❑	Insurance - Long Term Care	May be limited
❑	Insurance - Malpractice	
❑	Insurance - Property	
❑	Insurance - Worker's Comp	Employees only unless required by state
❑	Intangibles	Amortized
❑	Interest	Depends on type
❑	Internet Access	May be limited
❑	Inventory	Deducted as sold
❑	Investment Expenses	Not deductible
❑	IRA	Limited
❑	Janitorial Service	
❑	Kickbacks	Only if legal
❑	Land Purchase	Not deductible
❑	Land Lease	
❑	Landscaping	Not for Home-based Businesses
❑	Late Charges	
❑	Laundry Service	Limited
❑	Lawn Care	Not for Home-based Businesses
❑	Lease Payments	Depends on type
❑	Legal Fees	May be limited
❑	Leasehold Improvements	Depreciated
❑	Licenses	Depends on type
❑	Limousine Service	May be limited
❑	Loan Payments	Not deductible
❑	Loan Fees	
❑	Lobbying Expenses	Limited
❑	Lodging	May be limited

❑	Loss on Disposal of Assets	May be limited (Related Parties)
❑	Machinery	Depreciated
❑	Magazines	Business Related
❑	Mailing Lists	
❑	Mailing Supplies	
❑	Maintenance	Depends on type
❑	Manufacturing Costs	Depends on type
❑	Market Research	Depends on type
❑	Marketing Costs	May be limited
❑	Materials and Supplies	Depends on type
❑	Meals	Limited
❑	Medical Expenses	Very Limited
❑	Medical Savings Accounts	
❑	Meetings	May be limited
❑	Membership Fees	Depends on type
❑	Messenger Service	
❑	Mileage	May be limited
❑	Miscellaneous	Limited
❑	Motorcycle	Depreciated
❑	Moving Expenses	Not Meals
❑	Music System	Depreciated
❑	Net Operating Losses	May be limited
❑	Newsletters	Business Related
❑	Newspapers	Business Related
❑	Occupational Licenses	
❑	Office Equipment	Depreciated
❑	Office Expenses	
❑	Office Rent	
❑	Office Supplies	
❑	Organizational Costs	Amortized
❑	Outside Services	
❑	Packaging Materials	May be part of inventory costs

❑	Parents on Payroll	
❑	Parking	
❑	Parking Tickets	Not deductible
❑	Parties	May be limited
❑	Patents	Amortized
❑	Payroll	
❑	Payroll Services	
❑	Payroll Taxes	
❑	Penalties	Not deductible
❑	Periodicals	Business Related
❑	Permits	
❑	Personal Property Tax	
❑	Plants	
❑	Points - Loan	Over life of the loan
❑	Political Contributions	Not deductible
❑	Post Office Box	
❑	Postage	
❑	Prepayment of Expenses	May be limited
❑	Printing	
❑	Prizes to Customers	
❑	Profit Sharing Plans	Corporate only
❑	Promotional Expenses	
❑	Property Taxes	
❑	Protective Clothing	
❑	Publications	Business Related
❑	Real Estate Taxes	
❑	Referral Fees	
❑	Refunds	Reduce Income
❑	Reimbursements	Depends on type
❑	Renovations	Depreciated
❑	Rent	Depends on type
❑	Repairs	
❑	Reproduction	

❑	Research	Depends on type
❑	Restoration	
❑	Retirement Plans	May be limited
❑	Royalties	
❑	Safe Deposit Box	
❑	Safety Equipment	
❑	Salaries	
❑	Sales Returns	Reduce Income
❑	Sales Tax Collected	Not deductible
❑	Sales Tax Paid	Part of cost of purchase
❑	Samples	
❑	Security Services	
❑	Security Systems	Fees expensed; System depreciated
❑	Self Employment Tax	Special Rules apply
❑	Seminars	
❑	Service Contracts	
❑	Severance Pay	
❑	Sewer Service	
❑	Shipping Costs	
❑	Spouse on Payroll	
❑	Software	Depends on type
❑	Start-up Costs	Amortized
❑	State Taxes	
❑	Stationery	
❑	Storage Costs	
❑	Subcontractors	
❑	Subscriptions	Business Related
❑	Supplies	Depends on type
❑	Surety Bond	
❑	Surveys	
❑	Tariffs	
❑	Tax Penalties	Not deductible
❑	Tax Return	May be limited

	Preparation	
☐	Taxes - Federal Income	Not deductible
☐	Taxes - Local	
☐	Taxes - Payroll	
☐	Taxes - Property	
☐	Taxes - State	
☐	Telephone	Limited for Home-based Businesses
☐	Thefts	May be limited
☐	Tickets	Depends on type
☐	Tips	May be limited
☐	Tolls	
☐	Tools	Expensed or Depreciated
☐	Tractors	Depreciated
☐	Trade Show	
☐	Trademark	Amortized
☐	Trailers	Depreciated
☐	Training	May be limited
☐	Transportation	May be limited
☐	Travel	
☐	Trucks	May be limited
☐	Tuition	May be limited
☐	Unemployment Insurance	
☐	Unemployment Taxes	
☐	Unsalable Goods	
☐	Uniforms	
☐	Union Dues & Meetings	
☐	Use Tax	
☐	Utilities	
☐	Vacation Facilities	May be limited
☐	Vandalism	Not covered by Insurance

❑	Vehicles	May be limited
❑	Wages	
❑	Warehouse	Expensed or Depreciated
❑	Web Site	
❑	Worthless Goods	
❑	Yellow Pages	
❑	Zoning	

Small Business Deductions – A's

Keep in mind that all business expenses must be *ordinary, necessary and reasonable*.

ACCOUNTING FEES –
a. Accounting and tax preparation fees that you pay on an on going basis <u>are deductible</u> as a business expense.
b. Accounting fees that you pay when investigating a new business may or may not be deductible depending on what type of business you are in currently.
- i) If you are investigating a new business that is the same type as the business you are already in, the accounting fees <u>are deductible</u> as an expense if you end up not acquiring the new business.
- ii) If you are investigating a new business that is not the same type as the business you are in currently and you do not end up acquiring the new business, the accounting fees <u>are not deductible</u>.
- iii) If you pay accounting fees in investigating a business and end up acquiring the business, the accounting fees are considered 'Start Up Costs' and <u>are deductible.</u> Up to $5,000 of start up costs can be deducted in the year the business is started. An amount over that must be written off over a period of 60 months. It does not matter if you are currently in business or what type of business.

ADVERTISING –
All costs of advertising your business <u>are deductible</u>. This includes publicity and promotional type expenses.

AIRFARE –
Generally airfare is a deductible business expense provided the travel is for a genuine business purpose. Documentation must be provided as to the dates of travel, the name of the destination and the business reason for the travel or the business benefit gained or expected to be gained.

The airfare is deductible even if you stay at your destination for extra days for personal reasons. If you fly to Orlando for a business meeting and stay a few extra days to go to Disney, the airfare is still deductible. The *primary reason* for the trip, though, has to be business.

If you take your spouse and kids with you on your business trip, their airfare is only deductible if:
- they are an employee of your business,
- they have a bona fide business purpose in traveling with you **and**
- their expenses would be otherwise deductible.

ALARMS –
a. The cost of an alarm system itself is depreciated over the life of the alarm, generally 7 years.
b. The on going fees for monitoring the alarm system <u>are deductible</u>.

ALLOWANCE FOR BAD DEBTS – Actually the allowance for bad debts is the offsetting account we use to take a deduction for bad debts expense. It is used to reduce your Accounts Receivable. The allowance account represents how much of your Accounts Receivables you do not expect to collect.

46

Allowance for Bad Debts only applies to those that use the Accrual method of accounting and extend credit to their customers.

AMORTIZATION –
Amortization works similar to depreciation, but applies to intangible assets. Intangible assets are those things a business owns that have value but have no physical presence such as copyrights, patents, non-compete agreements and goodwill. They usually involve some kind of rights. Intangible assets are written off over a period of time specified by the IRS depending on their type.

ANSWERING SERVICE -
The fees you pay to your answering service <u>are deductible</u>. An answering machine or system would be depreciated.

ANTIQUES –
a. If you are in the antiques business, purchases would be counted as Inventory when bought and expensed as Cost of Goods Sold when sold.
b. If you purchase antiques to decorate your business, the cost is generally <u>not deductible</u> and is not eligible for depreciation. The IRS looks at this as an investment rather than an expense of the business.

APPRAISAL FEES –
Generally, appraisal fees become part of the cost (or basis) of whatever you are having appraised. Most of us are most familiar with appraisals of real estate. If you purchase property, real or personal, and pay for an appraisal as part of the purchase process, the appraisal fees become part of what that property cost you to

acquire it. Your cost then is depreciated over the life of the property or becomes part of the gain or loss calculation when you sell it.

ASSESSMENTS –
What we are talking about here are tax assessments on your real property made by a local governing authority, generally your city or   county. They show up on your property tax bill. Their deductibility is determined by what type of assessment they are.
   a. If the assessment is for repairs, the cost is deductible.
   b. If the assessment is for improvements, such as new sidewalks or curbs and gutters, the cost is not deductible, but becomes a part of the cost (basis) of your property.

ASSOCIATION MEMBERSHIP DUES –
Whether or not association membership dues are deductible depends on what type of association it is.
   a. If it is a business or trade association, the dues are deductible.
   b. If it is an association for entertainment purposes only, the dues are not deductible.

ATHLETIC CLUB MEMBERSHIPS –
Athletic club membership costs are not deductible.

ATTORNEY FEES –
   a. Attorney fees for matters associated with your on going business are deductible.
   b. Attorney fees associated with starting your business, such as drawing up a partnership agreement or incorporation papers, are considered 'Start Up Costs'. Up to $5,000 of start up costs can be deducted in the first year of business. Any excess is then expensed over 60 months.

48

c. Attorney fees associated with acquiring a new business are treated the same as accounting fees incurred for the same reason. Please refer back to accounting fees for the treatment of these costs.

AUDITS –
The costs associated with defending yourself in an audit are deductible. These may include accounting and/or attorneys fees. This would include audits of any kind associated with your business. It would not necessary have to be an IRS audit, but would also include an audit by any state or local governing body. It would also apply to audits of the value of real or personal property if your business is taxed on these things. In this area of the country, businesses are taxed locally on the amount of their personal property (equipment, machinery, computers), so the amount to defend your business in an audit of this type is deductible.

AUTOMOBILE EXPENSES –
This is a very complex area of the tax law, so bear with me as we go through the rules.

Automobiles are considered 'Listed Property' by the IRS and are subject to special rules.

Basically you have two ways to calculate your business auto expenses:
    a. The Standard Mileage method, or
    b. The Actual Expenses method

Whichever method you choose you will need the following information, each year, to deduct expenses for the use of a business auto:
    • Total miles driven for the year
    • Total business miles driven for the year

- The date the vehicle was placed into service in the business
- Your basis (cost) in the automobile

Standard Mileage Method

This method is available for you to use whether you own the car or lease it.

The expenses <u>included</u> in the standard mileage business allowance are: Depreciation, Fuel, Insurance, Lease Payments, Maintenance, Oil, Registration Fees, Repairs and Tires.

Expenses <u>not included</u> in the mileage rate and deductible in addition to the mileage are: Business parking fees and tolls, personal property taxes, and interest on any vehicle loan.

The rules allowing you to use the standard mileage method are:

1) The vehicle may not be used for hire, such as a taxi.
2) Five or more vehicles may not be used at the same time, such as a fleet operation. You can use five or more vehicles at different times, such as when your car is in the shop and you use your spouse's or your children's car.
3) You cannot have claimed a deduction on the vehicle in a prior year for:
   a) ACRS or MACRS depreciation (the IRS depreciation rules)
   b) Section 179 expense (the IRS code section that allows you to expense

some items rather than depreciate them), or

    c) Any method of depreciation other than Straight Line over the estimated useful life of the auto.

Owned vehicle –
If you own your vehicle, the election to use the standard mileage method is generally made in the year the vehicle is placed in service.

You can switch to the Actual Expense method in a later year, but you will have to calculate how much basis is left in your vehicle. Part of the Standard Mileage rate (51 cents per mile before 07/01/2011 and 55.5 cents on and after 07/01/2011, predicted to be the same for 2012) is considered to be for depreciation (22 cents per mile for 2011, 23 cents per mile for 2012). If the vehicle has been fully depreciated, no further depreciation may be claimed. If the vehicle is not considered fully depreciated, the Straight Line method must be used based on the remaining estimated useful life of the vehicle.

If you continue to use the Standard Mileage method after your vehicle is fully depreciated, the rate per mile remains the same, but none of it is considered as applying toward depreciation. The IRS's reasoning behind this is as the vehicle gets older the amount of deprecation decreases, but the amount of repair costs increases.

Leased vehicle –
If you elect to use the Standard Mileage method on a leased vehicle, you must use this method for the entire lease period of the vehicle.

Actual Expense Method

You must use the Actual Expense method if you have claimed depreciation on the vehicle in a prior year using any of the methods under standard mileage rule number 3 listed above.

Actual expenses include: Depreciation (with limits), Fuel, Insurance, Lease Payments, Maintenance, Oil, Registration Fees, Repairs and Tires. Only the business portion of each of these expenses is deductible.

Business miles include:

1. From one work location to another, such as from one job to a second job, from your office to a client's office or from your main business location to a temporary work site.
2. From home to a temporary work site. A temporary work site is one where the work is expected to last and actually does last for one year or less. Daily commuting expenses are allowed in going between a taxpayer's home and work location if:
   a. The expense is for going between the taxpayer's home and a temporary work location outside the metropolitan area were the taxpayer lives and normally works.
   b. The taxpayer has one or more regular work locations away from home and the expenses are for gong between home and a temporary work location, regardless of distance, or
   c. **The taxpayer's home is the taxpayer's principal place of business, and the expenses are for going between home and another work location, regardless of whether the other work**

**location is regular or temporary and
regardless of the distance.**
***One good reason to have a home
office!***

Nondeductible Business Miles

1. You cannot convert nondeductible business miles to deductible miles by conducting business in your car, such as making business calls on your way to work.
2. Expenses incurred in nonprofit carpooling to and from work are nondeductible commuting expenses. Any amounts received are considered a reimbursement and are not included in income. If operated for a profit, the payments received are income and the expenses are deductible (you would have to use the actual expense method as your vehicle would be considered to be for hire).
3. Travel costs to a remote location for an indefinite period whether they are for vehicle expenses or other travel methods (train, plane, etc.).

Records Required

You must keep certain records to be able to deduct business vehicle expenses. These include:
1. The amount of each expense for the vehicle including purchase price, improvements, lease payments, repairs and maintenance, fuel and any other expenses.
2. The total mileage on the vehicle each year and a breakdown of the business, personal and commuting miles, and
3. The date of each expense or use and the business reason for each expense or use of the vehicle.

I keep a small notebook in my vehicle to record the date, beginning and ending mileage, the client name and business purpose for each trip.

You do not have to keep mileage records for any vehicle that is unlikely to be used for personal reasons such as a delivery truck, ambulance or bus.

Small Business Deductions – B's

Keep in mind that all business expenses must be *ordinary, necessary and reasonable*.

BAD CHECKS –
When a check you received from a client is returned to your business and you are unable to recover the money, the amount of the check and any bank charges or other costs associated with trying to collect the debt is deductible as long as the income was included in your gross income.

BAD DEBTS –
The amount of uncollectible debt is deductible as long as it is associated with your business and you use the accrual method of accounting. In order to be deductible, the income associated with the bad debt must have included in the business records. If you are a cash basis taxpayer, income is not included in your income until it is received. If you never reported the income, you cannot deduct the bad debt. Bad debts are generally deductible only when totally worthless.

BAIL BOND FEES –
May be deductible if business related – remember the ordinary and necessary requirement though. Bail bond fees are not legal fines or legal penalties, which are non-deductible.

BANK CHARGES –
Fees charged by your bank on your business accounts are deductible. These would include service charges, charges associated with bad checks (yours or your customers), and credit card settlement fees.

BANKRUPTCY –
Costs associated with filing bankruptcy on your business
are deductible. On the down side, if you have debts
dismissed for expenses you previously deducted, you will
have to include this amount in your income. If you had
gone to Office Depot and charged supplies for your
businesses and deducted those expenses on your tax
return, then filed for bankruptcy and included the debt to
Office Depot, you would have to report income equal to
the amount of debt you will not pay because you received
a tax benefit from the expense at the time of purchase.

BENEFITS FOR EMPLOYEES –
Generally the cost of benefits you provide to your
employees are deductible. Deductible benefits include
accident and health plans, group-term life insurance (up
to $50,000 of coverage each) and dependent care
assistance programs.

**Planning Point: If you are a sole proprietor and
your spouse is a bona fide employee (providing
legitimate services to the business), the cost of
their coverage is deductible and you (as the
business owner) can be covered as a dependent
under their plan, making your coverage 100%
deductible**.

In addition to being a bona fide employee, your spouse
must meet the participation rules of a medical
reimbursement plan established by the business, cannot
be a joint owner, co-owner or partner in the business and
the insurance must be in the name of the employee-
spouse, not in the name of the employer-spouse.

WARNING: If the business is an S-corporation and one
spouse owns more than 2%, the other spouse is also
treated as owning more than 2% and not as an employee

for benefit purposes. So if an S-corporation pays health insurance premiums for either spouse, the benefit is taxable as wages (but not subject to Social Security or Medicare). However, it can be deducted as an adjustment to income on the front page of Form 1040.

BILLBOARDS –
The cost of billboards advertising the business is considered advertising and is deductible.

BONUS-EMPLOYEE –
Bonuses paid to employees are considered wages and are deductible. Bonuses are subject to Federal Withholding, Social Security and Medicare withholding just as regular wages are. I have seen many businesses give their employees 'cash' bonuses and fail to withhold taxes. This is NOT allowed and could get you in trouble with the IRS down the road.

BOOKKEEPING SERVICE –
If you use a bookkeeping service to keep your business books and records, the cost is deductible. See Accounting Fees for more information.

BOOKS –
Books you buy to help you run your business are deductible. The books can address a wide variety of subjects such as marketing, management, or employees, for example.
*The cost of this book is deductible as a business expense!

BRIBES –
If the bribe in question is illegal it is not deductible. As far as I know, all bribes in the United States are illegal, but it is an accepted practice in some other countries. If

you are doing business in another country where bribes are legal, the cost is deductible.

BROKER'S FEES –
If the broker's fees are incurred in association with the purchase or sale of property, the fee's become a part of the cost (basis) of the property and become part of the depreciation calculation, if appropriate. If you use a broker to buy products, the cost becomes a part of the cost of the product and is deductible as a Cost of Goods Sold when the product is sold. If you use a broker to sell your products, those costs are deductible.

BUILDINGS –
Buildings are considered capital (or fixed) assets and are depreciated. Under the IRS rules residential buildings are depreciated over 27.5 years and commercial (non-residential) buildings are depreciated over 39 years.

The cost of the land is never depreciated. When you buy a building and land, you must divide the cost between the buildings and the land to determine how much can be depreciated. You can use any reasonable basis to allocate the cost between the land (non-depreciated) and the building (depreciated). I often use tax assessment records to calculate a percentage to use in the allocation.

BUSINESS CARDS-
The cost of your business cards is deductible. You can deduct them either as advertising or as printing costs or even office supplies.

BUSINESS GIFTS –
The deduction for business gifts is limited to $25 per recipient per year, not including any gift wrapping. When calculating the $25 limit, you do not have to count:

1. Items that cost you $4 or less and are imprinted with your business name and are one of many identical items you distribute (such as free pens or calendars).
2. Gifts of tangible personal property to employees for length-of-service or safety achievement costing $400 or less. If the award is part of an established written plan and does not discriminate in favor of highly compensated employees, the maximum is increased to $1,600.
3. Nominal holiday gifts other than cash such as a turkey or ham.

BUSINESS LICENSES –
The cost of obtaining business licenses or permits <u>are deductible</u>.

Small Business Deductions – C's

Keep in mind that all business expenses must be *ordinary, necessary and reasonable*.

CAMPAIGN CONTRIBUTIONS –
Contributions paid to political campaigns are <u>not deductible</u>.

CANCELLATION PENALTIES –
Penalties charged to your business for the cancellation of a contract <u>are deductible</u>. These would include a non-refundable deposit paid on a contract that was not completed.

CAPITAL ASSETS –
The cost of capital assets is generally <u>not deductible</u>. Instead the cost is expensed over the life of the asset using the process of depreciation. Capital assets are generally long-lived tangible property such as machinery, equipment, furniture, computers and buildings. Although, technically, even inexpensive items such as wastebaskets and staplers have to be depreciated, the common practice is to expense these types of items.

CARRYING CHARGES –
Carrying charges are considered interest and <u>are deductible</u>.

CARTONS –
If considered part of a product, the cost of cartons is originally counted as Inventory and expensed as Cost of Goods Sold when the product is sold. If the cartons are not part of the actual product they <u>are deductible</u> when purchased.

CASUALTY LOSSES –
If your business suffers losses from fire, storm, flood or other casualty, any amount not covered by insurance is deductible. This also includes theft, shoplifting and vandalism.

If the losses affect fixed assets that are being depreciated, the amount of the loss only applies to the part of the asset that has not been depreciated yet (also known as book value). For example, you have a machine that has been destroyed. You paid $10,000 for the machine and you have already taken $6,000 of depreciation. The amount that you can deduct is $4,000 less any insurance you receive. In some cases you may even end up with a gain! If your insurance company pays you $5,000 for the loss of the machine, you would end up with a $1,000 gain.

Inventory that is lost, stolen or destroyed should not be reported as a casualty loss. Instead the cost of the inventory is deducted as part of your 'cost of goods sold'. Some companies use the term 'shrinkage' to apply to this type of loss and keep a separate record of the costs to help manage their businesses.

CATALOGS –
Catalogs showcasing your products are deductible. If you spend a large amount on catalogs at the end of your tax year, you must list them as an asset and expense them in the year they will actually be used.

CHARITABLE CONTRIBUTIONS –
How charitable contributions are treated depends on what type of legal entity you have chosen for your business. If you are a sole proprietor, partnership or S corporation, charitable contributions will be reported on your personal tax return as an itemized deduction (Schedule A). If your business is a corporation, you can

take charitable contributions on your business return, but the amount is limited to no more than 10% of your net income. Excess contributions can be carried forward for 5 years but if they are not used within that time, the deduction is lost.

CHILD CARE –
Some child care expenses are deductible and some are not. We will cover this in the next chapter under Dependent Care.

CHILD ON PAYROLL –
You can hire your children and deduct their wages as a business expense. They must provide bona fide services to the business and you cannot pay them more than you would pay someone else to do the same work.

**If your child is under 18 you do not have to withhold (and match) Social Security or Medicare. In addition, you do not have to pay Federal Unemployment on their wages. You will have to withhold Federal Income Tax from their wages if they make enough to have to pay taxes – generally the amount of the standard deduction for their filing status.

** **PLANNING NOTE**: You can pay your child for services on the business payroll and put the money into a traditional IRA for them, making up to $5,000 a year exempt from Federal Income Taxes. So, you could pay a child up to $10,700 (for 2011 & 2012) if they are single and put the maximum amount in a traditional IRA. They would owe no Federal Income Tax and be saving for the future!

CLEANING SERVICE–PREMISES –
The cost of having someone come in and clean up your business is deductible whether you pay them wages or a flat fee to an outside service.

CLEANING SERVICE-CLOTHING –
Only clothing that is unsuitable for street wear is deductible (such as uniforms); likewise, only the cost of cleaning clothing that is unsuitable for street wear is deductible.

CLOSING COSTS –
If the closing costs are associated with the purchase of property, they generally become the cost of the property increasing its cost (basis). The cost is then treated appropriately by being depreciated, expensed or held for investment and taken into account upon the sale of the property.

CLOTHING-WORK -
This deduction is very limited. Only clothing considered unsuitable for street-wear is deductible such as uniforms. Any clothing that you could (whether you do or not) wear for any purpose other than work (street wear) is not deductible.

CLUB MEMBERSHIPS –
Only club memberships that are for business clubs (Kiwanas, Lions and Rotary for example) are deductible. Club memberships where the club is for entertainment purposes are not deductible, such as golf or health clubs. Legitimate business meals at golf and country clubs are deductible, even though membership is not.

COFFEE SERVICE –
If you pay a coffee service for the rental of a coffee machine and re-stocking of coffee supplies, the cost is

deductible. If you purchase a coffee machine, it may be expensed or subject to depreciation depending on the cost.

COLLECTION COSTS –
Costs paid to an individual or service to collect monies owed to you are deductible.

COMMISSIONS –
Commissions paid to sales persons to sell your products are deductible. If you are required to pay a commission or fee in order to acquire property, the cost generally becomes part of the cost of the property and needs to be treated appropriately (depreciated, expensed or held until the property is sold).

COMMUTING EXPENSES -
Except for a very few situations (see Automobile Expenses), commuting expenses are not deductible.

PLANNING NOTE – If your business is a considerable distance from your home you have a couple of options to convert your mileage from nondeductible to deductible. You can get a P.O. Box close to your home and then make a stop to check to mail on the way to the office every day. Alternatively, you can make a call on a client or another business related stop before going to the office. Only the mileage between your home and your first business stop is nondeductible. This alone can save you thousands in taxes each year. The additional recordkeeping is well worth the deduction

COMPENSATION-EMPLOYEE –
Salaries, wages and commissions paid to your employees are deductible. If your business is a corporation (S or C) and you pay yourself, those costs are also deductible on the business level (you must give yourself a W-2 and

claim the income on your tax return). The business's share of the payroll taxes are also deductible.

** Compensation must be reasonable for the services provided to the company. This area has recently come under close scrutiny from the IRS, especially for closely held corporations. You want to make sure that your pay, and any relative's, is neither too much nor too little for the services provided. A good measure of what is reasonable is what you would have to pay someone else to do the same job.

COMPUTERS –
Business computers are most often <u>depreciated</u> or may be expensed in limited circumstances.
The problem with most of us, especially if we have a home office, is we use our computers for both business and personal. If this is the case in your situation, you must keep a log of hours the computer is used for business and the hours it is used for personal. Only the percentage of the computer that is used for business is deductible (whether depreciated or expensed).

EXAMPLE: You spend $2,000 on a new computer system. You use the computer for business and to check and send personal e-mail and keep your personal checkbook. Your kids also use the computer for games and school projects. You keep a log of the hours and purpose of computer use. The business use comes up to 60% at the end of the year. You can depreciated or expense (in certain circumstances) $1,200 of the computer's cost ($2,000 x .60).

If the computer is used away from your business premises, the computer must be used more than 50% for business in order for you to be allowed a deduction.

CONFERENCES –
The cost of attending or conducting business conferences are deductible. Traveling to and from the conference and lodging during the conference are also deductible (with a few exceptions). Meals are 50% deductible. More on these subjects to come under 'Meals' and 'Travel'.

The cost of your spouse attending the conference with you may also be deductible if they work for you in your business and there is a business reason for them to attend the conference.

CONSIGNMENT –
Consignment is goods that your business places with other businesses for them to try to sell. Let's say you make and sell widgets. You contact Widgets R Us and work a deal with them where you provide them with your widgets and they do not have to pay you for them unless, and until, they sell.

In this situation, no taxable (or deductible) event occurs until your widgets sell. Until a sale is made, you keep the cost of the widget in your inventory. Once a sale is made, you will record the sale to Widgets R Us and the corresponding movement of the cost of the widget from your inventory to cost of goods sold.

CONSULTANTS –
The costs you pay to consultants to help you run your business are deductible.

CONTESTS –
The cost of prizes awarded in contests run by your business to promote your business are deductible.

CONTRACTORS –
Fees paid to contractor's or sub-contractor's for the construction of business assets such as buildings are considered part of the building and are depreciated.

Minor work or repairs are deductible.

CONVENTIONS –
The cost of attending business conventions are deductible. See Conferences above.

Attending conventions outside the U.S. or aboard cruise ships are subject to stricter rules as to the amount that is deductible. More on this under Travel.

COPYRIGHTS –
A copyright is considered an intangible asset. Intangible assets are things that have value but no physical substance. They usually involve some kind of rights, such as with a copyright, patent or trademark. Intangible assets are written off over a period set by the IRS and the process is called

Amortization. Amortization is the intangible asset's equivalent to Depreciation for fixed assets.

If the cost of obtaining a copyright is small, it may be deducted at the time it is incurred.

COST OF GOODS SOLD –
If your business deals in physical goods, you will have two accounts that work hand in hand. One of these accounts is Inventory and is reported on your Balance Sheet as an asset of the business. Your Inventory account holds the cost of all of the items you have for sale to your customers. It does not affect your taxable income.

The other account is Cost of Goods Sold and it is reported on your Profit and Loss statement. Cost of Goods sold is a special expense account. It represents the amount you paid for those items that you have sold to your customers, hence "Cost of Goods Sold".

When you make a sale two transactions occur:
1. You make a sale, increasing your Sales (Income) account and your Cash account.
2. The cost of the item is moved from Inventory to Cost of Goods Sold.

The difference between what you sold the item for and what you bought the item for is called your 'Gross Margin' or 'Gross Profit'.

EXAMPLE: You make your widgets for a cost of $4.00 and sell them for $10.00. Your Gross Margin is $6.00 ($10.00 - $4.00). This is the money you have available to pay all of your other business expenses and provide a profit.

COSTUMES –
The cost of clothing used exclusively for work AND unsuitable for street wear is deductible.
The cost of cleaning is also deductible.

If you wear jeans and T-shirt to work, the cost is not deductible. If you have to dress up as a pumpkin for work, the cost of the pumpkin costume is deductible. If you have to wear a suit or dress for business and never wear them outside of business, the cost is still not deductible because you *could* wear them at other times, even if you don't.

COUPONS –
The cost of printing and distributing coupons for your goods or services <u>are deductible</u>. As the coupons are redeemed by your customers you can either record a lower sales price in your Sales account or record the sale at the regular amount and use another separate account to record the 'expense' of the discount the coupon offers.

Using the lower sales price is easier, but using the separate account allows you to track how much of a discount you have given to customers over a period of time.

COURIER SERVICE –
If you use a courier service for business purposes, the cost <u>is deductible</u>.

CREDIT CARDS –
Business purchases you make with a credit card <u>are deductible</u>. Any fees and interest charged for the use of the credit card are also deductible.

You can use your personal credit card for business purchases. The business items purchased are still deductible, but the fees and interest must be prorated between business and personal purchases and only the portion for the business expenses can be deducted. To make this easier, you can designate one personal credit card for business transactions only. That way, all of the costs associated with that particular card are deductible as business expenses and you don't have to do the pro-ration calculation.

If your business offers your customers the option of purchasing your goods or services with a credit card, all fees and charges associated with offering this option are deductible. These charges would include discount charges, statement fees, terminal rental or purchase and software rental or purchase.

CUSTOMS FEES –
Customs fees, duties and tariffs <u>are deductible</u>. Also any fees charged by international handlers or customs brokers are deductible.

In some cases, these costs should be included in your Inventory costs as part of the cost of the goods you sell and expensed to Cost of Goods Sold as sales take place.

Small Business Deductions – D's

Keep in mind that all business deductions must be ***ordinary, necessary and reasonable***.

DECORATING –
The costs of decorating your office or work space <u>is deductible</u>. Some large ticket items such as furniture would be subject to depreciation rather than expensed in the year purchased.

Remember, antiques are looked at by the IRS as an investment and the purchase of these types of items is not deductible as an expense or subject to depreciation.

DELIVERY CHARGES -
Delivery charges, to send or receive goods, <u>are deductible</u>.

There are two possible exceptions to this rule.

1. Delivery charges for the purchase of inventory are generally added to the cost of the inventory. Remember, inventory is held as an asset on the balance sheet until it is sold. At the time of sale, the cost of the inventory sold is moved from the Inventory account on the balance sheet to the Cost of Goods Sold account on your Profit and Loss statement.
2. Delivery or freight charges for equipment you purchase for your business are generally added to the cost of the equipment. The cost of the equipment, plus taxes, licenses, freight, installation and any other costs of getting the equipment in place and up and running are added together and become the basis (cost) of the equipment that is then subject to the rules of depreciation.

DEPENDENT CARE–
The cost of providing dependent care for your employee's children is deductible. You can pay for the dependent care directly or you can pay your employees up to $5,000 a year, tax-free, for them to pay for dependent care. Either way, your company gets the deduction.

DEPLETION –
Depletion is similar to depreciation in that it is a method to expense assets over their useful lives. Depletion is the name for the process used to expense natural resources such as coal, oil or timber and is generally calculated using a per unit method.

DEPOSITS –
Whether a deposit is deductible or not, depends on the type of deposit.

A non-refundable deposit is deductible.

A refundable deposit is not deductible. Rather, this type of deposit actually becomes part of the cost of whatever the deposit was on. A deposit on a piece of equipment, becomes part of the cost of the equipment. A deposit on an advertising order, becomes part of the cost of that advertising campaign. A utility deposit or security deposit is carried on the balance sheet as an asset as it is assumed that you will get it back one day.

DEPRECIATION –
Depreciation is the name for the process that allows a business to write off (expense) the cost of long-lived assets over a period of years. There are many different rules for the depreciation process. We will just cover the very basics here. You should contact your tax professional for more information on your particular situation.

The two things you must know to calculate depreciation are the cost (basis) and the estimated useful life of the asset.

The cost of the asset includes all costs for the purchase, delivery and set up of the asset. Included would be costs such as sales tax, licenses, freight, delivery and set up charges.

The IRS has established class lives for most assets ranging from 3 to 39 years. Most equipment falls in a 5-year or 7-year class life.

The two most common methods for depreciation allowed by the IRS are straight-line depreciation and MACRS (Modified Accelerated Cost Recovery System).

Straight-line depreciation is just what the name applies – your expense each year is the same – it is a straight line. To calculate straight-line depreciation, you take the cost (basis) of the asset and divide it by the number of years of useful life to get the annual expense amount.

MACRS is a system developed by the IRS and is based on a double-declining balance method of depreciation. Basically what this means is that the amount of depreciation expense is higher (approximately double of the straight-line amount) in the early years of an asset's life and declines as the asset ages. The IRS has numerous tables that are used to calculate each year's depreciation expense for each class life of assets. These tables can be found in IRS Publication 946 "How to Depreciate Property".

The other item of information that is needed to calculate the correct depreciation amount is when during the year the asset was placed in service. There are what we call 'conventions' that determine the amount of depreciation for the first and last year of an asset's life.

Generally, most assets are depreciated using a half-year convention. In the first year an asset is placed in service, you get a half-year's worth of depreciation. You also get a half-year in the last year of the asset's useful life. So, a 5 year asset would actually have depreciation expense in 6 years – half a year the first year followed by 4 full years and then a half a year in the last year, totaling 5 years.

There is also a mid-quarter convention that you can use. The only time this method is required is if you place more than 40% of all assets placed in service that year in the last quarter of the year (October 1 through December 31). In this case you MUST use the mid-quarter convention for all assets placed in service that year.

For example: if you purchased and placed in service $10,000 of assets in one year, but $5,000 of these assets were purchased and placed in service in December, you would be required to use the mid-quarter convention for all of the $10,000 worth of assets. And, I am sure you have guessed by now, the assets placed in service in the last quarter will have the lowest amount of depreciation as they only get one quarter's worth in the first year.

Most business people use the IRS's MACRS depreciation as it gives them the highest depreciation expense the quickest, but you can use straight-line depreciation if you chose. Some people like this method as it is simple to calculate.

There are a couple of instances where you are required to use straight-line depreciation. If you have real property (buildings) you are required to use straight-line depreciation.

For residential rental property, the useful life used to calculate depreciation expense is 27.5 years. For non-residential (commercial) property, the useful life is 39 years. You are also required to use a mid-month convention for real property. And, remember, you cannot depreciate the land the buildings stand on, only the buildings themselves.

You will need to use straight-line depreciation if you are using actual expenses for automobile expenses and intend to switch to the standard mileage method in the future.

For 2011, there is a bonus depreciation provision in effect. You can deduct (or expense) 100% of the adjusted basis of 'qualified property' to the cost of assets placed in service in 2011. They have to be brand new, used assets don't qualify. So if you bought a $12,000 piece of equipment, you can immediately write off the whole $12,000, but you will not have any write off available for future years for that piece of equipment. You do have the choice of electing out of the bonus depreciation.

There is depreciation in a nutshell, but before we leave this subject, let's talk about Section 179 expense for just a minute.

Section 179 is the section of the tax law that allows a business to expense a certain amount of assets rather than writing them off over their useful lives. This is the code section that caused so much attention in the media the last couple of years as applies to purchasing and writing off certain vehicles (SUV's).

Under current law, a business may expense up to $500,000 of assets purchased in one year, with some limits.

Limits to the Section 179 rules:
1. For every dollar over $2,000,000 of assets placed in service in any one year, there is a dollar reduction in the allowed Section 179 expense. By the time a business has placed $2,500,000 of assets in service, they no longer qualify for any Section 179 expense.
2. Husband and wife are treated as one taxpayer – together they can take a maximum of $500,000 in Section 179 expense rather than $500,000 each.
3. Qualifying property must be used more than 50% for business in the year placed in service. The annual depreciation limits for business autos still applies (more on this in a minute).
4. **Section 179 expense is limited to your taxable income from the active conduct of a trade or business. You cannot use the Section 179 expense to create a loss.** That said, the IRS has defined active trade or business income to include the trade or business of being an employee. What does this mean to you? If you have a part-time business and also work as an employee, you can use the 179 deduction to create a loss in your part-time business that will offset your income from wages! Or use the Section 179 deduction to create a business loss to offset your spouse's wage income.

NOTE ON AUTOMOBILES:

Most automobiles (those 6,000 pounds or less gross vehicle weight) are what the IRS calls 'Listed Property'. As such, there is a limit on how much depreciation you can take each year on your automobile. For 2011, the maximum depreciation was $3,060.

If you go out and buy yourself a Mercedes for $60,000, the most you can deduct for depreciation in any one year is $3,060.

BUT, there is a special little loophole in the IRS laws. If the 'loaded gross vehicle weight' is greater than 6,000 pounds, the vehicle is no longer considered a passenger auto and is not subject to the usual automobile depreciation limits.

If you go out and buy yourself a Hummer for $60,000, and you otherwise qualify for the Section 179 expense, **you can write off (expense) up to $25,000 in one year**! (It used to be 100%, but the law changed in 2005). See your tax professional to make sure you qualify.

DESIGN COSTS –
If the design costs are minor, they <u>are deductible</u> in the year they are incurred. Major design costs may have to be added to the basis (cost) of the item being designed and depreciated.

DIRECTOR'S FEES –
Director's fees, paid to corporation's board of directors, <u>are deductible</u>.

DISABILITY INSURANCE –
Disability insurance for your employees <u>is deductible</u>. If you are an employee of your corporation, your disability insurance is also deductible, but not for any other type of entity.

Insurance that pays your business overhead costs if you are disabled is deductible, no matter what type of business entity is used.

DISCOUNTS –
Discounts offered to your customers are generally shown as a reduction of your income rather than an expense of the business.

Purchase discounts, usually offered for prompt payment, are usually treated as a reduction of the cost of the purchased items. You may want to track this in a separate account to keep track of how much in discounts you are taking advantage of.

DISPLAYS –
The deductibility of displays for your merchandise depends on the type of display. If it is a temporary display, such as those cardboard displays you sometimes see in stores, and it is expected to last less than one year, you can deduct the cost.

More permanent displays, expected to last more than one year, would be subject to the depreciation rules.

DIVIDENDS-CORPORATE –
Dividends that a corporation pays to its shareholders are not deductible. Dividends are generally how a regular corporation distributes its profits to its owners and are not an expense of the business. Any costs associated with the actual distribution process are deductible.

DRAWS –
Money that an owner draws out of the business for personal use is not deductible. These amounts would be the corporate equivalent of a dividend.

DRIVEWAYS –
If you are maintaining an existing driveway, the cost would be <u>deductible</u>.

If you are building a new driveway, the cost would be subject to the rules of depreciation.

DUES –
Dues paid to a business group or a professional organization <u>are deductible</u>. If any part of the dues are used to influence politics (lobbying) that part is not deductible.

Some so-called business clubs are actually clubs run for pleasure, recreation or social purposes in disguise. Be careful, dues to these types of organizations are not deductible, even if you use them for business purposes.

Small Business Deductions – E's

Keep in mind that all business deductions must be ***ordinary, necessary and reasonable***.

EDUCATION EXPENSES –
Education expenses to maintain or improve a skill necessary to your business <u>are deductible</u>. The education must be directly related to your current trade or business.

Education expenses that are required to meet minimum education requirements or that qualify you for a new trade or business are <u>not deductible</u>.

Education expenses include tuition, fees for courses, books, laboratory fees, and travel costs if away from home overnight.

Examples:
Classes to improve your computer skills to help you run your business are deductible.

Classes to take the test required to become a real estate agent (and you are not a real estate agent now) are not deductible.

Travel as an educational tool is, generally, not deductible.

If you pay job-related education expenses for your employees, the cost is deductible.

You can also pay up to $5,250 per employee per year in non-job related education expenses and receive a deduction. These costs are not included in the employee's wages and are not subject to payroll taxes. If you are an employee of your corporation, you also qualify for this benefit, but not if you have any other type of entity.

ELECTRICITY –
The costs of electricity and other utilities for your business location(s) are deductible.

Home Based Businesses are subject to special rules. See the chapter on the Home Office Deduction.

EMPLOYEE BENEFITS –
Deductibility depends on the amount and type and are addressed individually.

EMPLOYEE BUSINESS EXPENSES –
If you reimburse your employees for out-of-pocket expenses, the cost is deductible. The reimbursed amount is not included in the employee's wages unless the reimbursement is more than the actual expenses. In that case, the excess is considered wages to the employee and should be included in their wages and taxed accordingly.

EMPLOYMENT AGENCIES –
If you use an employment agency to find workers for your business, the fees are deductible.

ENTERTAINMENT EXPENSES –
Entertainment expenses are limited to 50% of the cost. There can be a fine line between what qualifies as entertainment and what does not. The cost to a dress shop of putting on a fashion show is a 100% deductible expense while a party after the show would be a 50% entertainment expense.

This is one of the most scrutinized deductions, especially if you have a large amount of entertainment expenses. Remember, there must be a business purpose involved before, during or after the entertainment.

If you have a business meeting with a client then take them to a ball game, the cost of the tickets would qualify as an entertainment expense and be deductible at 50% of face value. The cost to get to and from the event and parking at the event are 100% deductible.

Any deduction for tickets to an entertainment event is limited to the face value of the tickets, even if you paid more than face value for them.

A company party where all employees and/or customers are invited is 100% deductible.

An item must be directly related to the active conduct of your trade or business to be deductible as an entertainment expense. There is a four-part test to establish whether an item is directly related to the active conduct of your trade or business:

1. You must have a more than general expectation of getting some income or specific trade or business benefit, other than goodwill, from making the expenditure;
2. During (or immediately before or after) the entertainment you actively engaged (or intended to engage but was prevented by circumstances beyond your control) in a business discussion, meeting, negotiation or other bona fide business transaction for the purpose of obtaining a specific business benefit;
3. It was reasonable for you to expect that the active conduct of trade or business would be the principal character or aspect of the entertainment; and
4. The expenditure was for the entertainment of your self and a person or persons from whom you reasonably expected a business benefit.

EQUIPMENT –
Most equipment is subject to the rules of depreciation.

ESTIMATED TAX PAYMENTS -
Estimated tax payments are not deductible. Federal
income taxes are never deductible. State income taxes,
the actual amounts, are deductible for federal income tax
purposes.

EXCISE TAXES –
Excise taxes are deductible.

Some states have a business income tax called an excise
tax. These taxes are deductible for federal income taxes,
but, generally, are not deductible for state income tax
purposes.

EXPENSE ACCOUNTS –
Whether or not expense accounts are deductible depends
on what the expenses are. See employee business
expenses above.

EXPORTING FEES –
Any fees charged for exporting your goods are deductible.
Such costs may include tariffs, duties, customs brokers or
international handlers. Legal bribes are deductible.

EXTERMINATORS –
Fees paid to exterminators are deductible. Special rules
apply to Home Based Businesses – see the chapter on the
Home Office Deduction.

Small Business Deductions – F's

Keep in mind that all business deductions must be ***ordinary, necessary and reasonable.***

FIDELITY BOND –
The cost of a fidelity bond for you or your employees <u>is deductible</u>.

FINANCE CHARGES –
Finance charges are <u>usually deductible</u>. We will talk more about this under Interest.

FINDER'S FEES –
Finder's fees are similar to commissions and <u>are deductible</u>.

FINES –
Fines for breaking the law are <u>not deductible</u>.

Fines for transactions that do not break any laws, such as a fine for not meeting contract obligations, <u>are deductible</u>.

FIRE PROTECTION SYSTEM –
Monthly or other recurring charges for fire system monitoring <u>are deductible</u>.

The cost of the system itself is generally depreciated.

FIRST AID SUPPLIES –
Any first aid supplies for your business <u>are deductible</u>. These costs would include a formal first aid kit as well as bandages, aspirin and other first aid supplies.

FIXED ASSETS –
The term 'fixed assets' refers to those items your business owns that provide benefit for more than one year.

Included would be buildings, equipment, machinery, furniture, fixtures and similar items that your business uses to produce an income. It would not include anything that your business sells.

Fixed assets are generally depreciated.

FIXTURES –
Fixtures refer to the items set up on the inside of your office or shop that are not an integral part of the structure such as shelves, display systems, coolers, etc.

Fixtures are generally depreciated.

FLOWERS –
The cost of flowers <u>is deductible</u> whether they are for a client, customer, employee or just to spruce up the office.

FOOD -
Food samples that are available to the public <u>are deductible</u>. Food and beverages served at a business-related event such as a convention or trade show or an open house are deductible.

Business meals are only 50% deductible and then are subject the specific IRS rules. We will learn more under 'Meals'.

FORFEITURES –
If a deposit or advance payment is forfeited under the terms of a contract, the cost <u>is deductible</u>.

FRANCHISE FEES –
Fees paid to a franchise to become a dealer, licensee, or distributor are generally amortized (expensed) over a period of time, currently 15 years, with a mid-month convention.

On-going franchise fees are deductible, in full, in the year paid or incurred.

FRANCHISE TAXES –
Franchise taxes are imposed by a state on a corporation for the privilege of doing business in that state. Some states also tax other business entity types such as limited liability companies.

Franchise taxes are deductible on your federal income tax return, but not, generally, on your state income tax return.

FREELANCERS –
If you pay someone outside of your business for services, freelancers, the cost is deductible.

NOTE: If you pay a person or unincorporated business (partnership or limited liability company) more than $600 a year for services, you are required to give them a Form 1099 at the end of the year and report the amount paid to each person or business to the IRS by providing them with a copy of the 1099.

FREE SAMPLES –
Any free samples given out to customers or potential customers are deductible at your cost. You cannot deduct the 'sale price' of the items given, only your cost.

You cannot deduct the value of your services given out for free. If your business is a corporation and you are an employee of that corporation, the wages you are paid while performing free services are deductible.

FREIGHT –
Freight charges for sending or receiving goods <u>are deductible</u>, with two exceptions:

1. Freight paid to receive inventory is added to the cost of your inventory and kept on your Balance Sheet until sold.
2. Freight paid to receive machinery or equipment becomes part of the cost or basis of that piece of machinery or equipment and is depreciated.

FRINGE BENEFITS –
Fringe benefits you provide to your employees <u>are generally deductible</u> with some exceptions and limits.

Each type of fringe benefit, such as awards, gifts, health insurance, life insurances and medical expenses is addressed individually.

FUEL –
If used for a business purpose, fuel for automobiles, boats and aircraft <u>are deductible</u>.

Heating fuel <u>is deductible</u>.

FURNITURE –
Furniture used in your business is an example of fixed assets. Fixed assets are generally depreciated.

Small Business Deductions – G's

Keep in mind that all business deductions must be *ordinary, necessary and reasonable*.

GARBAGE SERVICE –
Garbage service, whether regular or periodic, <u>is deductible</u>.

GARDENING EXPENSES –
Gardening, landscaping and lawn care expenses <u>are deductible</u>, whether you pay a service or hire someone on your payroll.

Gardening, landscaping and lawn care expenses are <u>NOT deductible for a home-based business.</u>

GIFTS – BUSINESS –
The deduction for business gifts is limited to <u>$25 per recipient per year</u>, not including any gift wrapping. When calculating the $25 limit, you do not have to count:

4. Items that cost you $4 or less and are imprinted with your business name and are one of many identical items you distribute (such as free pens or calendars).
5. Gifts of tangible personal property to employees for length-of-service or safety achievement costing $400 or less. If the award is part of an established written plan and does not discriminate in favor of highly compensated employees, the maximum is increased to $1,600.
6. Nominal holiday gifts other than cash such as a turkey or ham.

GOODWILL –

Goodwill, sometimes called 'blue sky' is the amount you pay for a business over and above the value of the assets you purchase with the business.

An established, on-going business is generally worth more than just the value of the assets you receive due to it having an established client base, on-going advertising, etc., that difference is called goodwill.

Goodwill is amortized (expensed) over a period of years, currently 15 years with a mid-month convention.

GRAPHIC DESIGN –
Graphic design costs for a short-term project are deductible.

Graphic designs for larger projects, such as those that become a part of your product, may have to be amortized over a period of years.

GREETING CARDS -
Greeting cards for your customers or employees are deductible.

GROSS RECEIPTS TAX –
Some local governing authorities charge a gross receipts (sales) tax. This is not the same as sales tax and is the sole responsibility of the business (it cannot be passed on to the customer).

Gross receipts taxes are deductible.

GROUP HEALTH INSURANCE –
Group health insurance that you provide for your employees is deductible as well as reimbursements under a medical reimbursement plan.

NOTE: If your business is any type of an entity other than a C corporation, health insurance to cover yourself may or may not be 100% deductible. Current tax law allows you to deduct 100% of your own health insurance on your Form 1040 if the amount of the insurance is less than the net income from your business. If the insurance is more than your business net income, you can deduct the cost of the insurance on your Schedule A, Itemized Deductions, but your total medical expenses must be more than 7.5% of your Adjusted Gross Income and you must itemize to take advantage of this deduction.

Planning Point: If you are a sole proprietor, a partnership, or a limited liability company hire your spouse (they must be a bona fide employee) and provide health insurance for them with you as a member covered under their insurance plan. Their coverage is 100% deductible to the business regardless of the business net income.

Note: This will not work for an S corporation if you are a more than 2% shareholder. The IRS looks at you **and your spouse** as owning more than 2% of the business in this case and you are back to falling under the self-employed health insurance rules. Your health insurance may still be 100% deductible.

If your business is a C corporation and you are an employee of the business, your heath insurance is 100% deductible to the corporation.

GUARD DOG –
The cost of feeding and maintaining a guard dog is deductible.

The cost of the dog itself would be depreciated.

Be careful to make sure you have a true business purpose for requiring a guard dog. The family pet will generally not qualify as a 'true' guard dog.

GUN –
Like the guard dog, if you have a true business for requiring a gun, you can depreciate the cost of the gun. You can also deduct the expense of lessons to learn how to handle and shoot the gun.

Small Business Deductions – H's

Keep in mind that all business deductions must be *ordinary, necessary and reasonable*.

HEALTH INSURANCE –

1. Sole Proprietors, Partners, Members of LLC's, and S Corporations Shareholders:

Up to 100% of your own health insurance <u>may be deductible</u>. Self-employed health insurance is deducted on the front page of your Form 1040 as an adjustment to income, NOT on your business return. Why is this important? Because your self-employment tax (15.3%; 13.3% for 2011 and the first 60 days of 2012 as of this writing) is calculated on your business return, so you are paying with your insurance in 'after tax' dollars.

Also, your self-employed health insurance deduction is **limited** by the income of your business (under which the plan is established). If you are in a break-even or loss situation, your health insurance premiums are then moved to your Schedule A, Itemized Deductions. At this point, the total of all of your medical expenses must exceed 7.5% of your Adjusted Gross Income and you must qualify to itemize to get any tax benefit at all.

Plus, **you do not qualify** to take the deduction if you are eligible (only eligible, whether you participate or not) to received employer paid or subsidized health coverage from your employer (if you have another job) or through your spouse's employer.

2. Employee Health Insurance – including C corporations owner's who are also employees:

Health insurance for your employees, their spouses and dependents are 100% deductible.

Payments to employees under an established medical reimbursement plan are also 100% deductible.

Neither payments are included in the employee's income. All employees must be eligible to participate in the coverage plan.

3. Family Employees:

If you employ your family members, spouse, children or parents, they are eligible for the same 100% deductible coverage that all of your employees are. If you fall under category 1, above, you can hire your spouse and be covered under their policy to achieve 100% deductible health insurance coverage.

WARNING: Your family members must be bona fide employees performing legitimate work. Generally the IRS looks at whether or not you would have to hire and pay someone else to do the jobs that your family is doing. It is a good idea to have an employment contract, outlining duties, with your family members – and all of your employees for that matter.

HOBBY LOSSES –
If the IRS, not you, determines that your activities are a hobby rather than a legitimate business, you must include any income on your tax return, but you are NOT allowed to deduct any losses. As a matter of fact, you must include all income and the deductibility of any expenses is very limited!

See Chapter 2, "Business versus Hobby – Why Should I Care?" for more information.

HOME DEMONSTRATIONS –
If you give demonstrations of your products or services in your home, any out-of-pocket expenses for literature, decorations, samples and/or refreshments <u>are deductible</u>.

HOME OFFICE –
You are allowed, subject to rules and limitation, to deduct a portion of your home expenses if you are conducting a business out of your home.

Please see the Chapter: "The Truth About the Home Office Deduction – The Best Thing Since Sliced Bread or Not?" for complete and detail information on this deduction.

HOUSING ALLOWANCE –
Housing allowances given to your employees that qualify as ordinary and necessary <u>are deductible</u>.

In order for the housing allowance to be deductible and tax free to the employee, three conditions must be met:

1. The lodging provided must be for the convenience of the employer, not the employee, and
2. It must be a required condition of employment, and
3. It must be on the employer's premises.

Think of a resident manager of an apartment building-they would meet all three conditions.

Small Business Deductions – I's

Keep in mind that all business deductions must be ***ordinary, necessary and reasonable***.

ILLEGAL EXPENSES –
Any expenses for illegal purposes are <u>not deductible</u>.

NOTE: By law, drug dealers are only allowed to deduct their Cost of Goods Sold. I wonder how many drug dealers file legitimate tax returns?

IMPORTING COSTS –
Any costs to import products <u>are deductible</u>. This may include taxes, tariffs, duties or charges from brokers or handlers.

Some costs may be required to be added to inventory costs and deducted as cost of goods sold when the product is actually sold.

IMPROVEMENTS –
Major improvements to any asset that extends its life or increases the value is generally added to the value of the property and depreciated.

Minor repairs and maintenance <u>are deductible</u>.

INCOME TAXES –
Federal income taxes are <u>never deductible</u> except on a very few state returns.

State income taxes <u>are deductible</u> on your federal income tax returns, but not usually deductible on the state return.

INCORPORATION FEES –
Fees you pay to incorporate, including state fees, attorney and accounting fees, are written off (expensed) in the year of formation, up to $5,000. Any excess amount would be deducted over 60 months.

INDEPENDENT CONTRACTORS –
Independent contractors are people or unincorporated businesses that sell their services to other businesses. The fees you pay to independent contractors are deductible or depreciated depending on what type of services they are providing.

See the chapter on Employee versus Independent Contractor for more information.

NOTE: If you pay a person or unincorporated business (partnership or limited liability company) more than $600 a year for services, you are required to give them a Form 1099 at the end of the year and report the amount paid to each person or business to the IRS by providing them with a copy of the 1099.

INSURANCE –
Generally, any insurance you buy for business purposes is deductible. There are certain types of insurance, however, that have special rules:

1. Automobile Insurance is deductible only if you use the actual expense method. See Automobile Expenses.

2. Worker's Compensation Insurance on your employees is deductible. If you are self-employed, worker's compensation insurance on yourself is only deductible if your state requires that you carry it.

3. Disability insurance on employees is deductible. Disability insurance for yourself is only deductible if you are an employee of your corporation.

4. Life Insurance on employees is deductible as long as the employer (you) are not the beneficiary of the policy. If your employees have life insurance with coverage of more than $50,000, the amount of the premium for the coverage over $50,000 is included in the employee's wages and is subject to the normal payroll taxes.

   You cannot deduct the life insurance on yourself if you are a self-employed individual (sole proprietor, partner, limited liability member or S corporation shareholder). If you are an employee of your corporation, you are covered by the rules above.

5. Business interruption insurance may or may not be deductible depending on exactly what the insurance covers.

   If the insurance covers overhead when the self-employed individual is unable to work the premiums are deductible.

   If the insurance pays lost earnings to the self-employed individual while they are unable to work, the premiums are not deductible.

   If the insurance pays for lost profits while the business is shut down due to reasons covered in the policy (the most common is fire), the premiums are deductible.

INTANGIBLES –
Intangibles are those assets that have value but no physical presence and usually involve some kind of rights such as copyrights, patents and trademarks. Goodwill and a covenant not to compete are also intangibles.

Most intangibles are expensed (amortized) over 15 years. Software is expensed over 3 years unless its useful life is one year or less such as my tax software which changes every year.

INTEREST –
Most interest on business related debt <u>is deductible</u> except as noted below:

1. If the interest is paid on the construction of a fixed asset, such as a building, the amount paid during construction is added to the basis (cost) of the asset and then depreciated.

2. Points and origination fees on the purchase of real estate can be deducted when to property is purchased, but if you are refinancing, the points and fees must be deducted over the life of the loan.

3. Interest on back taxes is not deductible (except for corporations).

4. Prepaid interest (interest paid in advance of when it is due) is not deductible until the time it actually applies to; even cash basis taxpayers cannot deduct prepaid interest.

INTERNET ACCESS –
The cost for Internet access <u>is deductible</u> if it is used 100% for business purposes. If part of the use is

personal, fees must be allocated between the two and the personal part is not deductible.

You must keep a diary of hours used for business and hours used for personal. Using these figures, calculate the percentage of business use (business hours divided by total hours). Then apply the percentage to the total Internet access fees to find the deductible amount.

INVENTORY –
The cost of your inventory (products held for resale) is carried on your Balance Sheet and not deducted (expensed) until it is sold.

When you make a sale, there are actually two transactions that take place:
1. A sale is made – increasing your income account and your cash (or Accounts Receivable) account.
2. The cost of the product(s) sold is moved from your Inventory account to your Cost of Goods sold account.
3. The difference between these two amounts (Sales Price less Cost of Goods Sold) is called your Gross Profit or Gross Margin. It represents the amount of money you have left from the sale to pay the expenses of running your business.

Most small business software packages will track these two simultaneous transactions for you.

You should always take a physical inventory at least once a year. It does not even have to be at the end of the year as long as it is about the same time every year.

Your cost of goods sold can also be calculated as follows:

```
    Beginning Inventory
  + Purchases
    Goods Available for Sale
  - Ending Inventory
    Cost of Goods Sold
```

Some businesses add all of the inventory they buy to their Purchases account (a type of cost of goods sold account) and then calculate their actual Cost of Goods Sold after they take a physical inventory at the end of the year.

INVESTMENT EXPENSES –
Expenses for brokers fees, investment publications, consultants, investment advice and such are not deductible as business expenses. The IRS does not consider investing a business. You may be able to deduct some or all of these expenses on your Schedule A, Itemized Deductions.

IRA –
Contributions to Individual Retirement Plans are not deductible as a business expense. They may be deductible on your Form 1040 depending on the type of IRA, your income levels and whether or not you are covered by a retirement plan at another job.

More on IRA's when we look at Retirement Plans.

Small Business Deductions – J's

Keep in mind that all business deductions must be ***ordinary, necessary and reasonable.***

JANITORIAL SERVICE –
Janitorial and/or cleaning services <u>are deductible</u>.

Small Business Deductions – K's

Keep in mind that all business deductions must be *ordinary, necessary and reasonable*.

KICKBACK'S –
The term 'kickback' can cover all sorts of different payments from illegal bribes to rebates to customers or payments for referrals. Deductibility depends on the type of kickback you are dealing with.

Legal kickbacks are deductible, illegal kickbacks are not.

Small Business Deductions – L's

Keep in mind that all business deductions must be *ordinary, necessary and reasonable*.

LAND –
The purchase of land is <u>never deductible</u> or depreciated. The cost of land is 'held' on your books until you sell it, then the cost is used to calculate any gain or loss on the land.

LAND LEASE –
If you lease land for your business, the lease payments <u>are deductible</u>.

LANDSCAPING –
The cost of landscaping your business premises <u>is deductible</u>.

No landscaping charges are deductible for a home-based business.

LATE CHARGES –
Late charges <u>are deductible</u>, except for late payment charges on government forms and tax returns.

LAUNDRY SERVICES –
If your business requires the use of laundry services, such as a hotel, the costs <u>are deductible</u>.

Laundry costs for uniforms not suitable for street wear <u>are deductible</u>.

Laundry costs for clothing that is suitable for street wear are <u>not deductible</u>, even if you only wear the clothing for business purposes.

LAWN CARE -
Lawn care costs for your business premises <u>are deductible</u>.

No lawn care costs are deductible for a home-based business. The IRS figures you are going to have to mow your lawn whether you have a business there or not.

LEASE PAYMENTS –
Lease payments for business buildings, machinery, equipment, automobiles, etc. <u>are deductible</u> in most cases.

If your lease is structured more as a purchase than an actual lease, then the item(s) leased need to be treated as though they were purchased. A lease will be considered a purchase if there is a bargain purchase option at the end of the lease. If you retain ownership of the item at the end of the lease for a payment of little or no money, it should be treated as a purchase.

Automobile Leases – are not 100% deductible, you must add back an "Inclusion Amount" that is calculated by the IRS and based on the fair market value of the vehicle at the time it was leased. See a competent tax professional for more information. The 'Inclusion Amount' does not apply to vehicles with a loaded Gross Vehicle Weight of over 6,000 pounds.

LEGAL FEES –
Legal fees are generally <u>deductible</u>. See Attorney fees for more information.

LEASEHOLD IMPROVEMENTS –
Improvements made to leased business property are generally <u>depreciated</u>. This would include items such as walls, shelves, displays and counters.

LICENSES –
The costs of licenses (including professional licenses) to do business <u>are deductible</u>.

Automobile licenses are deductible under the actual expense method, but not the standard mileage method.

If you have other business property that requires a license, the costs are deductible.

LIMOUSINE SERVICE –
If there is a business purpose for the hiring of a limousine service, the cost <u>is deductible</u>.

If it can be considered an entertainment expense, only 50% is deductible.

LOAN PAYMENTS –
When you take out a loan, for business or personal reasons, the proceeds from that loan are not included in your income. Likewise, when you pay back the loan, the part of the payments that is applied to the loan principal is <u>not deductible</u>.

If the loan is for business purposes, the interest portion of the payment is deductible.

LOAN FEES –
The costs of obtaining a loan, such as points and closing costs, <u>are deductible</u>, but must be spread out over the life of the loan.

LOBBYING EXPENSES –
Any amounts paid for political purposes are <u>not deductible</u> including any part of the cost of a membership

in an association that is used for political lobbying purposes.

There are three exceptions to this rule:
1. Expenditures made to influence local (city or county) legislation are deductible.
2. Expenditures used to only monitor legislative activities are deductible.
3. Annual in-house expenditures up to $2,000 are deductible. Not included are any amounts paid to professional lobbyists and any part of dues paid to an association that are used for lobbying purposes. If the in-house expenditures exceed $2,000 then none of the expenses are deductible.

Contributions to a political campaign are <u>not deductible</u>.

LODGING –
Lodging expenses when traveling away from home on business <u>are deductible</u> with some limits. We will delve further into this subject when we discuss travel.

Also see the discussion under Housing Allowance if you are providing lodging to your employees.

LOSS ON DISPOSAL OF ASSETS –
A loss on the disposal of an asset <u>is deductible</u>, provided the sale or other disposal was an "arms length" transaction.

In other words, you cannot sell your assets to a related party at a discount just to generate a loss.

The loss is calculated as the difference between the sale price and the basis of the asset.

Basis would be calculated as the cost of acquiring the asset less any depreciation allowed and/or taken.

Example:

Three years ago you purchased a piece of machinery for $10,000. You have taken depreciation of $6,000 on the machine as of the date of the sale. You sell the machine for $3,000. You have a $1,000 loss on the sale of this machinery, calculated as follows:

Basis: $10,000 cost less $6,000 of depreciation taken = $4,000 basis

Sale price of $3,000 less basis of $4,000 = $1,000 loss on disposal of your asset.

Small Business Deductions – M's

Keep in mind that all business deductions must be ***ordinary, necessary and reasonable***.

MACHINERY –
Most machinery must be depreciated.

MAGAZINES –
The costs of subscriptions to magazines or other business publications <u>are deductible</u>.

There must be a business purpose to the subscription.

MAILING LISTS –
The costs renting or purchasing mailing lists <u>are deductible</u>.

MAILING SUPPLIES –
Mailing supplies for your business <u>are deductible</u>, as well as the cost of mailing.

MAINTENANCE –
Minor maintenance and repair costs <u>are deductible</u>.

Major maintenance projects that add to an asset's life, increase capacity or add to the value of the asset may have to be depreciated.

MANUFACTURING COSTS –
Accounting for manufacturing costs is its own world. Basically, anything that becomes part of a product is assigned to the cost of that product including part of overhead costs. Other costs, not directly associated with or assigned to a product, <u>are deductible</u>.

MARKET RESEARCH –
Market research costs for short-term projects <u>are deductible</u>.

Market research for a long-term project, one that will benefit more than one year, should be deducted (expensed) over the life of the project.

MARKETING –
Marketing is a term that can cover a wide variety of activities including advertising, promotions, publicity, entertainment, mailings, catalogs, just to name a few.

Most marketing expenses <u>are deductible</u>, some may have to be expensed over a period of time depending on the specific campaign. Entertainment expenses are only 50% deductible.

MATERIALS AND SUPPLIES –
Materials and supplies used to run your business <u>are deductible</u>.

Materials and supplies that become part of a product must be included in that products inventory costs and not expensed until the product(s) are sold.

MEALS –
Regular meals at work are <u>not deductible</u>.

Meals with a business purpose, such as meeting with a client or an associate, <u>are 50% deductible</u>. You must keep a receipt and write on it: who the meal was with and the business purpose for the meal.

The cost of the meal cannot be lavish or extravagant. You are not suppose to deduct the cost of alcoholic beverages, either, just the cost of the food itself.

Meals while traveling away from home for a business purpose are also 50% deductible.

Meals you provide to your employees on your business premises for your convenience are 100% deductible. There must be a clear business purpose for providing the meals such as requiring the employees to be on call, attend a lunch meeting or working overtime.

Occasional meals provided to employees, such as a party or picnic, are 100% deductible.

WARNING: Say you are out driving around, calling on your clients. It is lunchtime and you are hungry, so you wheel into you local fast food joint and grab a burger and fries. Is this meal deductible? Answer: No. If you are eating alone, without a client or potential new client, meals are only deductible if you away from home overnight.

MEDICAL EXPENSES –
The cost of reimbursing your employees for medical expenses for them and the members of their families under an established medical reimbursement plan are deductible. If you are an employee of your C corporation you would fall under these rules.

If you have an unincorporated business or an S corporation, you cannot deduct your own medical expenses on your business return. Those with an unincorporated business may employ their spouses and be covered under their reimbursement plan. S corporation shareholders cannot deduct their medical expenses through their business whether they employ their spouses or not.

MEDICAL SAVINGS ACCOUNTS –
Contributions to medical savings accounts are <u>not business deductions</u>, rather they are deducted on the front page of Form 1040 as an adjustment to income.

There are specific rules to the use of MSA's. See IRS publication 969 "Medical Savings Accounts" for more information.

MEETINGS –
The costs of business meetings <u>are deductible</u>. The costs of meals are only 50% deductible. If the cost of a business meeting includes the cost of a meal, and that meal cost is not separately identifiable, the general consensus at this time is that the entire cost is 100% deductible.

MEMBERSHIP FEES –
Membership fees for business clubs, trade associations and professional organizations <u>are deductible</u>. Any portion of the membership fees that supports political lobbying is not deductible.

Membership fees in an organization of a recreational or entertainment purpose are not deductible. You golf club membership fees are not deductible, but if you take a client to there for a round of golf and a meal, the cost for the round of golf and the meal itself is 50% deductible.

MESSENGER SERVICE –
The cost of using a messenger service <u>is deductible</u>.

MILEAGE –
Refer back to Automobile Expenses on the rules for deducting mileage expenses.
MISCELLANEOUS –

Sometimes a business has costs that just don't fit into any other category of expenditure. You can use the miscellaneous category for these items, but be very careful that the total amount claimed as miscellaneous is small. Large miscellaneous deductions will red flag your return.

If at all possible, classify all expenditures as anything other than miscellaneous.

MOTORCYCLE –
The cost of a motorcycle to be used in your business would be depreciated.

MOVING EXPENSES –
The cost of moving your business from one location to another is deductible.

MUSIC SYSTEM –
The cost of a music system for your business is depreciated as long as it is not lavish or extravagant.

The cost of the music media (CD's, DVD's, Tapes) is deductible.

Small Business Deductions – N's

Keep in mind that all business deductions must be **_ordinary, necessary and reasonable_**.

NET OPERATING LOSSES –
Occasionally, your business may have a year where your expenses are more than your income, resulting in a loss. In some cases that loss may be used to offset income from other sources such as a job or a spouse's job. This reduces your overall tax liability for the year.

If your business losses exceed all income from other sources you may be able to carry the loss back to previous tax years, and receive a refund on money already paid in taxes. If the loss is carried back to as many years as are allowed and are still not used up, you may be able to carry the remaining loss forward to offset future income.

If the Net Operating Loss (NOL) occurred before 2001 or after 2002, you can generally carry the loss back two years and then forward 20 years. NOL's arising from 2001 and 2002 tax years are carried back five years and then forward 20 years. No matter what year that the loss was generated, you can elect not to carry any of the loss back and, instead, carry the entire loss forward 20 years.

Calculating NOL's and amending tax returns, if you carry back, can be very complicated. There are many rules to govern what qualifies as an NOL and how the carry back or carry forward is to be accomplished. You also want to make sure that, if possible, you carry the NOL to the highest income years. You should seek competent tax help if you have a loss situation.

NEWSLETTERS –
The cost of newsletters on business topics <u>is deductible</u>. The newsletters do not have to specifically deal with your

type of business, newsletters on general business subjects qualify.

NEWSPAPERS –
The cost of newspapers <u>is deductible</u>, as long as it is providing some benefit to your business.

NOTES –
Notes payable, such as those for the purchase of real estate or machinery and equipment for your business are <u>not deductible</u>. Principal payments are not deductible. Interest payments generally are deductible. See Interest.

Small Business Deductions – O's

Keep in mind that all business deductions must be ***ordinary, necessary and reasonable***.

OCCUPATIONAL LICENSES –
If you need a license to carry on your trade or business, the cost is deductible.

OFFICE EQUIPMENT –
Most office equipment must be depreciated.

OFFICE EXPENSES (or Office Supplies) –
'Office expense' is kind of a catch-all phrase for anything you purchase to help run your office. Items included in this category would include paper, pencils, pens, paper clips, markers, envelopes, glue, tape, stationery, first aid supplies, toner, cleaning supplies, etc. The list can be quite extensive.

All office expenses are deductible.

OFFICE SPACE -
If you rent your office space, the cost is deductible.

If you own your office building, the cost of the building is depreciated. Depreciation is 39 years for non-residential real estate. You can "split out" any separate costs and use a shorter depreciable life for things like carpet, some fixtures like shelving, and land improvements such as your driveway. All of these things have shorter depreciation periods that can be taken advantage of.

Home-Based businesses have special rules for the deduction of office space. See the chapter on The Home Office Deduction for more information.

ORGANIZATIONAL COSTS –

Up to $5,000 of organizational or 'start-up' costs can be deducted in the first year of business. Any amounts over this are expensed over 60 months starting the first month of business.

OUTSIDE SERVICES –
Outside services is another name for independent contractors. If you hire independent contractors to perform services for your business, the cost <u>is deductible</u>.

Remember that if you pay an unincorporated business more than $600 a year for services, you must provide them with a 1099. See Independent Contractors for more information.

Small Business Deductions – P's

Keep in mind that all business deductions must be
ordinary, necessary and reasonable.

PACKAGING MATERIALS –
Deductibility depends on type of packaging materials:

1. Packaging materials, including cartons, boxes or
    bottles, that become part of your product are
    counted as part of your cost of inventory and
    reported on the Balance Sheet until sold. Once the
    product is sold, all costs of that product is
    transferred from the Balance Sheet to the Income
    statement through the use of an expense account
    called Cost of Goods Sold. It is at this time that the
    cost becomes <u>deductible</u>.

2. Packaging materials that are used to ship, or
    deliver, your products to customers <u>can be
    deducted</u> as Postage and Delivery or Freight Costs.

PARENTS ON PAYROLL –
Unlike when you hire your children, there are no special
tax breaks for hiring your parents. You parents are
treated just like any other employee you would hire. The
only difference is that your parents wages are not subject
to Federal Unemployment Tax (FUTA) and may not be
subject to State Unemployment Tax (SUTA). Check with
your state department of labor for clarification.

Payroll costs are deductible.

PARKING –
The cost of parking <u>is deductible</u>, even if you use the
standard mileage method to calculate your automobile
expenses.

Parking tickets are not deductible, but towing charges are deductible.

You can deduct the amount your business pays for your employees to park on or near your business premises. If the amount per employee, per month is less than $200 (2005), the parking is considered a tax-free fringe benefit to the employees.

PARTIES –
The cost of a company party where all employees are invited is 100% deductible.

A sales meeting, show or exhibit where refreshments are served is 100% deductible as long as the primary purpose for the event is the conduct of business.

Business parties, lunches, dinner or other events that are primarily for enjoyment, even if business is conducted during the event, are considered entertainment and only 50% is deductible.

PATENTS –
Patents are called intangible assets as they have value but no physical substance. The cost of obtaining a patent, including attorney's fees, must be amortized (deducted) over 15 years beginning in the middle of the month that the costs were incurred.

PAYROLL –
Payroll expenses, including hourly wages and salaries, are deductible.

Bonuses, commissions, Christmas gifts are all part of your payroll. As such they are deductible, but they are also subject to payroll taxes. See Payroll Taxes below.

NOTE: Compensation amounts (how much you pay your employees) must be reasonable, neither too high nor too low. This is especially critical for employee-owners of corporations. To stay within a safe range, think about how much you would have to pay someone else to do your job.

PAYROLL SERVICES –
If you pay a service to calculate your payroll, print paychecks, pay your payroll taxes and/or file your payroll returns, the cost is deductible.

PAYROLL TAXES
The employer's portion, your share, of Social Security and Medicare taxes are deductible, as well as Federal Unemployment and State Unemployment taxes.

The employee's share of Social Security, Medicare, Federal and State Withholding is not deductible. These amounts are subtracted from the gross wages you are paying your employee, the amount of gross wages is deductible. You are simply acting as a tax collector for the government for the employee's share of payroll taxes.

If your business is a sole proprietorship, a partnership or a limited liability company, you (the owner) pay your share of your Social Security and Medicare taxes on your Form 1040 – through the use of Self-Employment taxes. You do get a deduction, on the front of your Form 1040, for one half of the Self-Employment tax.

WARNING – Time and time again, I see businesses that are struggling put off paying their payroll taxes. DO NOT fall into this habit – the fines and penalties are stiff and, eventually, the government will shut your business down. Put some other creditor on hold, but not the federal government!

A good habit to get into is to make your payroll tax deposit, through your bank or by electronic funds transfer, at the same time you do your payroll. First, you won't forget to make the payment and, second, you will not be tempted to spend the money on something else.

PENALTIES –
If the penalty is for violation of the law, local, state or federal, the penalty is <u>not deductible</u>.

If the penalty is for some other reason, such as failing to meet contract requirements, the penalty <u>is deductible</u>.

PERIODICALS –
Periodical is just another name for literature you receive periodically such as weekly, monthly, quarterly, etc. generally through a subscription. If the periodical is business related, the cost <u>is deductible</u>. It does not have to be specifically related to your type of business, it can relate to business in general and still be deductible.

PERMITS –
All business permits and licenses <u>are deductible</u>.

Construction permits generally become a part of the building, or other asset, and are depreciated over the proper time period.

PERSONAL PROPERTY TAX –
In the tax sense, personal property does not mean property that belongs to you personally.

In the business and tax world, basically there are two different types of property – real property and personal property. Real property consists of land and anything permanently attached to the land, such as building. Personal property is anything that is not real property.

Then there is personal use and business use. So you can have personal use real property and personal use personal property, or you can have business use real property and business use personal property.

Anyway, many jurisdictions (state and local) impose a personal property tax on business use personal property. This would include automobiles, furniture and fixtures, equipment – both manufacturing and office, and machinery – anything that is not real property and used in your business.

Personal property taxes <u>are deductible</u>.

PLANTS –
Plants used as office decoration, whether green and growing or silk, <u>are deductible</u>. The cost of upkeep for your plants is also deductible.

POINTS –
Points are part of the cost of borrowing money. One point equals one percent of the loan amount. Points and other loan origination fees are <u>deductible over the life of the loan</u>.

This is different from the points on the purchase of your personal home, which are deductible in full in the year of purchase. Points for re-financing your personal home, however, must be deducted over the life of the new loan.

POLITICAL CONTRIBUTIONS –
Political contributions to a campaign or a political party are <u>not deductible</u>.

Advertising in a political program or buying tickets to a political event are also not deductible.

POST OFFICE BOX –
Rental fees for a post office box, at the post office or mailbox rental store, <u>are deductible</u>.

POSTAGE –
The cost of postage and postal permits <u>is deductible</u>.

PREPAYMENT OF EXPENSES –
Technically, expenses <u>cannot be deducted</u> until the period (year) to which they apply. As a practice, though, businesses generally deduct the cost of minor prepayments for office supplies, a service contract, Internet access, etc. The IRS has not challenged this practice.

However, tax law specifically states that pre-payments on interest, business property rents, insurance and property taxes cannot be deducted until the period to which they apply. <u>This applies even if you keep your books on a cash basis</u>.

PRINTING –
The cost of printing, related to your business, <u>is deductible</u>.

This would include brochures, advertising, business cards, flyers, catalogs, etc.

NOTE: If you have a big printing order at the end of your tax year, that will primarily benefit the next tax year, you are suppose to carry the cost on your Balance Sheet at the end of the year and expense it the following year (the year to which it applies). See Prepayments above.

PRIZES –
Prizes to your customers or suppliers are deductible.

PROFESSIONAL ORGANIZATIONS AND
ASSOCIATIONS –
The cost of dues and meetings are deductible.

Meals at meetings are only 50% deductible.

PROFESSIONAL SERVICES -
Professional, consulting, accounting and legal services
are deductible.

PROFIT SHARING PLANS –
True profit sharing plans are only deductible for
corporations.

PROMOTIONAL EXPENSES –
All costs of promoting your business are deductible.

NOTE: Be careful of the fine line between what is a
promotion and what is an entertainment! If in doubt, it
is probably entertainment expense rather than
promotional expense.

PROPERTY TAXES –
Property taxes, on business property, are deductible,
whether they are imposed on real property or personal
property. See Personal Property Taxes above.

If you are a home-based business, and qualify to take the
home office deduction, you can write off a portion of your
home's property taxes. See the last chapter, "The Truth
About the Home Office Deduction – The Best Thing Since
Sliced Bread or Not?"

PROTECTIVE CLOTHING –
The cost of protective clothing, and the cost of cleaning, <u>is</u>
<u>deductible</u>.

This would include items such as safety glasses, jumpers
and steel-toed shoes.

PUBLICATIONS –
Books, magazines, newsletters, newspapers, CD's and any
other business related publications <u>are deductible</u>.

Small Business Deductions – R's

Keep in mind that all business deductions must be
ordinary, necessary and reasonable.

REAL ESTATE TAXES –
Real estate taxes are deductible. See Property Taxes.

REFERRAL FEES –
Fees paid for referrals are deductible.

REFUNDS –
Money refunded to a customer is deductible as long as
the sale has been included in income. Generally refunds,
along with returns and allowances, are shown in the
income part of a tax return as a reduction in income
rather than as an expense. The net effect is the same.

REIMBURSEMENTS –
If you are reimbursed for out-of-pocket expenses, most
people include the reimbursement in income and deduct
the expenses as regular business expenses.

If you are reimbursing an employee for out-of-pocket
business expenses, you are entitled to deduct the
expenses as if you had paid for them directly. The
amount of reimbursement is not included in the
employee's wages, taxes are not withheld and the amount
does not go on the employee's W-2 at the end of the year.

If the amount of reimbursement to the employee is more
than the actual expenses, the additional amount is
considered additional pay and is deductible as payroll
expense and subject to payroll taxes.

If the amount of the reimbursement to the employee is
less than the actual expenses, the employee may be able
to deduct the part of the expenses for which they were not

paid. The employee must itemize their deductions on Schedule A of Form 1040 and their non-reimbursed business expenses must be over 2% of their adjusted gross income. Then, only the amount over 2% is deductible.

Remember: The owner of a sole proprietorship, partnership or limited liability company is <u>never</u> considered an employee of the business.

RENOVATIONS –
Minor renovations, that do not add value or extend the life of an asset, <u>are deductible</u>.

Building renovations that add value to or extend the useful life of a building must be added to the cost of the building and depreciated.

Additions to buildings have their own useful life and are, generally, depreciated separately.

RENT –
Business rentals and leases, whether for real property, equipment, machinery or vehicles, <u>are deductible</u>. Prepaid rent cannot be deducted, however, it can only be deducted in the year to which it applies.

If you rent your home, you may be able to deduct part of the rent if you also qualify for the home office deduction. See the last chapter on the home office deduction for more information.

If you lease an <u>automobile</u> for more than 30 days, the entire lease is <u>not deductible</u>. The IRS has tables for an "Inclusion Amount" that details how much can and cannot be deducted. You can find the tables in IRS Publication 463. This rule does not apply to trucks, vans or heavy sports utility vehicles – over 6,000 pounds gross vehicle weight.

REPAIRS –
Repairs and maintenance on business property <u>is deductible</u>.

Major repairs may have to be capitalized and depreciated – see Renovations above.

REPRODUCTION –
Reproduction and printing costs <u>are deductible</u>.

RESEARCH –
The costs of conducting day to day research for your business <u>is deductible</u>.

If the research is part of the development of a product or process, it may have to capitalized and depreciated.

RESTORATION –
Generally, restorations are added to the cost of the asset and depreciated, especially if it adds to the value of the property or extends the life of the property.

RETIREMENT PLANS –
The rules covering retirement plans, and the plans themselves, are many and varied. This area is scheduled for a special report in the near future. I will let you know when the report is ready.

Retirement plan contributions an employer makes for employees <u>are deductible</u>.

REWARDS –
Rewards paid to customers, suppliers and other non-employees <u>are deductible</u>.

Rewards paid to employees are also deductible and, if the reward is less than $400, it is also tax free to the employee. If the reward is over $400, the entire amount is taxable to the employee as regular wages and subject to payroll taxes. If the plan doesn't discriminate in favor of highly compensated employees, the amount goes up to $1,600.

ROYALTIES –
Any royalties your business pays <u>are deductible</u>.

Small Business Deductions – S's

Keep in mind that all business deductions must be *ordinary, necessary and reasonable.*

SAFE DEPOSIT BOX –
Rental fees for safety deposit boxes <u>are deductible</u>.

If you keep personal items in the same box as business items, you must split the rental fees between the two. Rental fees for a personal safety deposit box are deductible, with some limits, on Schedule A of Form 1040.

SAFETY EQUIPMENT –
Safety equipment, including first aid kits and fire extinguishers, <u>are deductible</u>.

Large safety equipment, that would benefit more than one year, may have to capitalized and depreciated. An example of this would be a sprinkler system.

SALARIES –
Salaries you pay your employees <u>are deductible</u>. See Payroll for more information.

SALES REFUNDS OR RETURNS –
Money you give back to your customers as a refund or payment for returned items is <u>deductible</u> as long as the income was included in your gross sales.

In most cases, these amounts are reported on the tax return as a reduction in income rather than an expense. The net effect is the same.

If a customer returns an item and you can sell it again, the cost of the item must also be added back into your inventory and used to reduce your cost of goods sold.

SALES TAX –

Sales tax is neither income to your business nor an expense of your business. You merely act as a tax collector for the taxing authority.

If you are paying sales tax on purchases for your business, the tax becomes a part of whatever you have purchased. You do not have to track sales tax separately on your purchases.

For example, if you purchase fixed assets, such as furniture, fixtures or equipment, the sales tax becomes part of the cost of the asset and is then depreciated.

SAMPLES –

If you give out samples of your product to prospective customers, the cost (not the sales price) of the samples is deductible.

SCHOLARSHIPS –

Scholarships you give to your employees are deductible.

SECURITY SERVICES –

Security services and/or patrols are deductible.

Monthly monitoring fees paid to a security service are deductible.

The cost of the security system itself will, in most cases, have to be capitalized and depreciated.

SELF-EMPLOYMENT TAX –

Self-employment tax is imposed on the owners of unincorporated businesses such as sole proprietorships, partnerships and limited liability companies. This tax is a combination of the employer's and employee's share of

Social Security and Medicare. Since you are self-employed, you get to pay both sides of Social Security and Medicare.

Self-employment tax is calculated on the Net Profit from Schedule C of your Form 1040 for sole proprietors or on your share of the business profits if your business is a partnership or limited liability company (even if these profits have not been paid out to you) reported to you on Schedule K-1.

You do get a deduction on front page of your Form 1040, as an adjustment to income, for one-half of the self-employment tax.

You do not get a business deduction for self-employment taxes.

SEMINARS –
Most business seminars are deductible.

SERVICE CONTRACTS –
Service contracts and extended warranties are deductible.

Prepaid contracts can only be deducted in the year to which they apply, whether you are a cash or accrual basis taxpayer.

SEVERANCE PAY -
Severance pay that is paid to your employees as part of a separation package is deductible as payroll expense and subject to payroll taxes.

SEWER SERVICE –
Sewer charges are deductible, as are water charges.

Sewer assessments, if for repair of your sewer system, are deductible. If the assessments are for the construction of a new system, the cost would be capitalized and depreciated.

SHIPPING COSTS –
Shipping costs are deductible, unless they are part of the cost of receiving your inventory. In this case they are added to the cost of the inventory and expensed as the inventory is sold. See Freight for more information.

SHOWS –
The cost of putting on a show to promote your business is fully deductible, including any food or beverages served at the show.

Business shows that you attend are deductible, except the meals which are only 50% deductible.

SPOUSE ON PAYROLL –
You may hire your spouse as an employee of your business. As a matter of fact, it may even be a good idea to do so. Their wages are 100% deductible to the business and are subject to payroll taxes (except Federal Unemployment Tax and, perhaps, State Unemployment Tax).

If your spouse is legitimately employed in your business, they can receive 100% health coverage just as your other employees do. You can then be listed as a dependent of your spouse and receive coverage also. **This is true only for unincorporated businesses**. See Health Insurance for more information.

SOFTWARE –
Computer software is generally depreciated over three years.

If the software only has a useful life of one year, such as tax preparation software, you <u>can deduct</u> 100% in the year it is purchased.

START UP COSTS –
If you incur costs simply investigating what type of business you want to start, these costs are generally <u>not deductible</u>.

On the other hand, once you begin the process of starting a business, the costs incurred before the business actually opens are considered your start up costs. These may include things that you would expect such as accountant or attorney fees and incorporation fees, but they also include rent, telephone, advertising and printing costs. Basically any cost that you incur before you open your doors for business is considered a start up cost.

The IRS has argued that a business does not start until it has made its first sale, but it has been successfully argued that the business started once it is 'open for business' and trying to generate income.

Start up costs up to $5,000 can be expensed in the year your business started. Excess costs are expensed over a period of 60 months, beginning in the month you open your doors for business. One way to get around having all of your pre-start expenses designated as start up costs is to start on a very small scale, perhaps even from home. Then, when you have started generating revenue, look for a more suitable location and purchase your furniture and equipment. The feasibility of this, of course, depends on what type of business you are in.

There is more on this subject under Accounting Fees.

STATE TAXES –
There seems to be an endless list of state taxes on businesses. Property taxes and income taxes, which may be in the form of a franchise and/or excise tax, are probably the most common.

State taxes <u>are deductible</u>.

Exception: Sales taxes are not deductible, neither are they income. See Sales Tax above.

STATIONERY –
Stationary, envelopes and other office supplies <u>are deductible</u>.

STORAGE COSTS –
The rental of a storage facility <u>is deductible</u>.

The costs of moving goods in and out of storage are also deductible.

SUBCONTRACTORS –
Subcontractors, contract labor, independent contractors, outside services are all names for people who perform work for you, but are not employees. Generally you pay them by the job rather than by the hour.

The cost of subcontractors <u>is deductible</u>. If an individual or unincorporated business performs more than $600 in services for you in a year, you are required to give them a Form 1099 at the end of the year. This form notifies the IRS as to how much they have made so the IRS can make sure that all income has been reported. There are fines and penalties if you are required to provide 1099's to your subcontractors and you don't.

WARNING: I have seen many business owners pay their employees as subcontractors so they don't have to withhold and pay payroll taxes. This can be a BIG mistake. It is not what you decide your workers are – it is what the IRS says that determines whether your workers are employees or subcontractors. The fines for paying your workers as subcontractors when they are truly employees can be HUGE. See the chapter on Independent Contractors vs. Employees for more information.

SUBSCRIPTIONS –
Business subscriptions <u>are deductible</u>.

SUPPLIES –
Supplies <u>are deductible</u>.

If supplies become part of a product that you sell, they must be included as part of your inventory cost and then deducted as the products sell.

SURVEYS –
The cost of conducting a survey <u>are deductible</u>.

The cost of surveying land is considered part of the cost of the land and is added to the land basis. This basis is then used to calculate a gain or loss on the land when it is sold, and only then is the surveying costs recovered.

Small Business Deductions – T's

Keep in mind that all business deductions must be **_ordinary, necessary and reasonable._**

TARIFFS –
Tariffs, customs fees and duties <u>are deductible</u>. Fees charged by customs brokers and international handlers are deductible.

 In some cases, these fees should be added to the cost of your inventory and deducted as your products are sold (as Cost of Goods Sold).

TAX CREDITS –
Tax credits are special incentives enacted by Congress to encourage (or discourage) certain behavior or to stimulate the economy.

You might be familiar with the child tax credit Congress enacted in recent years. This was done to boost the economy and give families with dependent children a tax break.

I bring this matter to your attention because I want to show you the difference between a tax deduction and a tax credit. **Tax credits are much more valuable**.

A tax deduction reduces the amount of income that is subject to tax. Let's look at some examples:

 Say you have $40,000 in taxable income and are single. Using the 2009 tax rates, your tax would be $6,188.

 But you are entitled to some deductions, let's say $10,000 worth of deductions. That leaves you with $30,000 in taxable income and your tax would be $4,083. So your $10,000 in deductions saved you $2,105 or 21% of the amount of your deductions. To find the amount of taxes a deduction would save you, you simply multiply the amount of the deduction times your tax rate, in this case 21%.

A tax credit on the other hand, is a dollar for dollar reduction of your taxes. So let's say in addition to $40,000 in taxable income and $10,000 of deductions, you are also entitled to a $1,000 tax credit. Now your tax would be $3,083 ($4,083 - $1,000). The credit gives you a dollar for dollar reduction of the taxes you owe!

Tax credits come and go and the amounts available change from year to year. The IRS will not tell you if you are entitled to a credit and do not take it. They sure are quick to tell you if you owe more money though! If you discover you were entitled to a tax credit and did not take it, you have up to three years to file an amended return.

The most common credits available for 2011 included:

Child Tax Credit
Credit for Child and Dependent Care Expenses
Credit for the Elderly or Disabled
Earned Income Credit (for low income families with qualifying children)
Education Tax Credits (including the American Opportunity & Lifetime Learning Credits)
Foreign Tax Credit
General Business Credit – a combination of 19 different credits
Small Business Health Care Tax Credit – if you pay 50% or more of employees health insurance
Qualified Adoption Expenses
Retirement Savings Contributions Credit/Saver's Credit

See a qualified tax professional to determine which credits you are eligible to take – remember the IRS will not tell you.

TAX PENALTIES –
Tax penalties for non-payment or underpayment of taxes are not deductible.

TAX RETURN PREPARATION –
Tax return preparation fees for your business are deductible on the business return.

Tax return preparation fees for your individual taxes are deductible on Schedule A (Itemized Deductions) of Form 1040 as a Miscellaneous Expense subject to the 2% floor.

Note: If you are a sole proprietor filing a Schedule C along with your 1040, be sure your tax preparer splits their fees into business and personal amounts so you can deduct the business amount on Schedule C. Any competent tax preparer should already know to do this. If they don't know this, it may be time to find another tax preparer.

TAXES – FEDERAL INCOME –
Federal Income Taxes are not deductible.

TAXES – LOCAL, PAYROLL, PROPERTY AND STATE –
Generally, these taxes are deductible. See the individual tax listings for more information.

TELEPHONE –
All of your business telephone services, fees and taxes are deductible, including the business portion of your cell phone. If you use your cell phone for personal calls also, you must split the fees between non-deductible personal calls and deductible business calls.

Home-Based Businesses:
You cannot deduct the cost of the first phone line into your house. The IRS assumes you will have a phone in your home whether you have a business there or not. You can deduct the cost, including taxes, of any business long distance calls made on your home phone.

If you have a second line, for business purposes only, you can deduct 100% of the cost of this line. I even have the phone company send me a separate bill for my second line, so I can pay it out of my business account.

THEFTS –
The type of deduction, if any, you are entitled to for stolen property, depends on what type of property was stolen.

For fixed assets (property you are depreciating) you can take a theft loss for <u>the amount that has not been depreciated yet,</u> often referred to as basis. So if you have a piece of equipment that you bought a few years ago for $6,000 and you have taken, over the years, $4,000 in depreciation, your basis for the equipment is $2,000. If that equipment is stolen, you are only entitled to a maximum deduction of $2,000.

You must also subtract any insurance money you have been paid for the theft. It is possible you may end up with a gain and taxable income, rather than a loss! If your insurance company pays you $3,000 on the stolen equipment you actually have $1,000 of income! $2,000 basis - $3,000 insurance payment = a negative $1,000 deduction which equals a gain!

TICKETS –

Tickets to sporting, music, theater and similar events are considered entertainment and if purchased for a business purpose are 50% deductible. This deduction is based on face value only; if you pay a scalper more than face value for the tickets, you can only deduct 50% of the face value. See Entertainment for more information.

If you purchase tickets to give to a client, the purchase becomes a gift. Business gifts are deductible up to $25 per recipient.

Raffle tickets are generally considered donations and only C corporations can deduct donations (and then they are limited to 10% of taxable income). For any other type of entity, the cost of the contribution is reported on Schedule A of your individual 1040.

Parking tickets, speeding tickets and any other tickets for illegal actions are not deductible.

TIPS –

Tips paid for meal service are considered part of the cost of the meal and are only 50% deductible.

Tips for any other service, such as valet parking or taxi service, are fully deductible.

TOLLS –

Highway tolls are deductible.

If you take the standard mileage allowance for vehicle expenses, tolls are deductible in addition to the standard mileage.

TOOLS –
Tools that are inexpensive and/or have a useful life of one year or less are deductible.

More expensive tools and tools that have a useful life of more than one year are depreciated.

TRACTORS –
If you purchase a tractor for your business, the cost is generally depreciated.

TRADE –
Trade or barter transactions are taxable events. You must include the income from the trade in your gross receipts at fair market value. If the item you received in trade qualifies as a business expense, it is deductible at fair market value.

TRADE SHOW –
Admission fees to trade shows are deductible.

Travel to and lodging during a trade show is deductible. Meals are 50% deductible if away from home overnight.

TRADEMARK –
The cost of obtaining a trademark is amortized (expensed) over a 15-year period beginning in the month it is acquired.

If a trademark is acquired from another business, under a licensing agreement, the payments are deductible when paid rather than amortized.

TRAILERS –
Trailers that are purchased for your business are generally depreciated. Trailers are not considered

vehicles by the IRS, so do not come under the limitations for vehicles.

Mobile home trailers are considered real property and must be depreciated accordingly.

TRAINING –
Training seminars, videos, manuals, etc. <u>are deductible</u>. Be sure to refer back to Education Expenses for more information.

TRANSPORTATION –
Most transportation expenses <u>are deductible</u> except the trip from your home to your work, commuting expenses, which are not deductible. Another reason to have an office in your home!

If, during the drive to or from work, you make a side trip to a supplier or client, the expense or mileage for that side trip is deductible.

TRAVEL –
Local business travel, when not staying over night, is limited to transportation expenses only. Again, commuting expenses are not deductible.

You can deduct the costs of food, lodging and miscellaneous expenses only when you travel away from your home overnight. Please note – this is away from your business home – your place of business – not your personal home.

If you are always traveling and do not have a business home, none of your travel expenses are deductible. In this case, the IRS considers the road your business home, so you are never away from your business home and cannot deduct the expenses for meals, lodging or miscellaneous expenses.

TRAVEL WITHIN THE UNITED STATES –
Travel for 100% business within the U.S. is 100% deductible including round trip transportation, lodging and incidental expenses such as telephone, fax, copies, and laundry. Meals and entertainment during your business trip are 50% deductible.

Travel on cruise ships for a business convention or seminar is limited to $2,000 a year and must meet the following requirements: the ship is a US flagship and all ports of call are located within the US or its possessions.

TRAVEL OUTSIDE THE UNITED STATES –
If you make a business trip outside the U.S., the cost may still be deductible (meals and entertainment are still only 50% deductible and cruise limitations apply). If you attend overseas conventions, seminars or meetings, a deduction is allowed only if the meeting is directly related to your business and if, in the IRS's opinion, there is a valid business reason for holding the meeting overseas.

TRAVEL – COMBINING BUSINESS AND PLEASURE –
If the reason for your trip is primarily personal (more than half the days), none of the travel expenses to and from your destination are deductible. Only the expenses directly related to a business purpose are deductible.

If the reason for your trip is primarily business (more than half the days), the cost of traveling to and from your destination are deductible. Only the expenses, such as lodging, meals and entertainment, relating to the extra personal days are non-deductible.

If your business requires you to be at a location on Friday and again on Monday, you can deduct your expenses for the whole weekend including lodging, meals and entertainment. The only requirement is that it was cheaper to stay at your destination than it was to travel home on Friday and back on Monday.

NOTE: If you're combining travel for business and pleasure the rules are a little bit different. As long as the trip is no more than one week or the time spent for pleasure is less than 25% of the entire trip, the same rules as travel in the U. S. apply. But if the trip is more than one week, or if the vacation days are 25% or more of the trip, you must allocate the travel expenses between the business and personal portion of your trip.

A 'business day' does not require you do business all day. Any day you put in at least four hours of work is considered a business day. Any day your presence is required is also a business day. Travel days also count as business days.

For lodging, meals and incidental expenses you have a choice of keeping track of each expense or using standard per diem (per day) rates established by the IRS. IRS publication 1542 "Per Diem Rates" contains the per diem rates for all locations.

TRAVELING WITH ANOTHER INDIVIDUAL –
Generally if you take your spouse, children or any other individual on a business trip with you, you cannot deduct the additional expenses related to their travel. The only time travel expenses for another individual going with you on a business trip are when that individual:
- Is your employee or business associate,
- Has a bona fide business purpose in traveling with you, and
- Their travel expenses would be otherwise deductible.

So, if your spouse is your employee and you require their help with your business on your trip, their travel expenses are also deductible!

WARNING: **Because of the liberal way the tax laws are written concerning business travel, it is tempting for many small business owners, especially sole proprietors who don't have to answer to anyone, to write off vacation trips as business travel. Be VERY careful here. This is one point of contention with the IRS.**

Be sure that you have documentation of the business purpose of your trips, contacts made, types of business conducted, anything to further substantiate your business purpose for the trip. I may even go so far as to keep a log of my activities during each business day of the trip. While not required by law, it may help to convince the IRS of the legitimate business purpose for the trip.

TRUCKS –

Trucks are considered fixed assets and would, generally, be depreciated. Vehicles have special limitations. Refer back to Automobile Expenses for more information.

TUITION –

Some tuition is deductible – see Education Expenses for more information.

Small Business Deductions – U's

Keep in mind that all business deductions must be **_ordinary, necessary and reasonable._**

UNEMPLOYMENT INSURANCE –
The taxes that employer's pay for their employees for state (SUTA) and federal (FUTA) unemployment is <u>deductible</u>.

Sole proprietors, partners in partnerships and members (owners) of limited liability companies are not subject to federal unemployment insurance on their own business incomes. They may also be exempt from state unemployment insurance. Check with your state Department of Labor.

UNEMPLOYMENT TAXES –
Unemployment taxes and unemployment insurance are the same thing. Whichever term you use, they <u>are deductible</u>.

UNSALABLE GOODS –
When goods cannot be sold due to obsolescence or irreparable damage, they can be <u>deducted</u> as part of your Cost of Goods Sold.

UNIFORMS –
Uniforms used exclusively for work are <u>deductible</u>. This includes costumes and protective gear. The cost of cleaning uniforms is also deductible.

Clothing with your company's logo or advertising is considered a uniform and is deductible.

If you can wear clothing outside of work (what the IRS calls "suitable for street wear") the cost is not deductible. So, if you wear business suits to work and don't wear them anywhere else, they are still not considered uniforms and their cost is not deductible.

UNIONS –
The cost of union dues and union meetings is <u>deductible</u>.

If part of your union dues are for political lobbying, that portion of the dues is not deductible. Your union should provide you with a statement that breaks down what your dues cover.

USE TAX –
Use tax is the sales tax you are suppose to pay to your state for those taxable items you buy in another state that you did not pay tax on at the time you purchased it. Many people are not even aware of the use tax.

If I go on the Internet and buy my office supplies from Joe's Wholesale Supply, they do not charge me sales tax because my business is not in the same state as Joe's. What I am suppose to do is include the cost of these out state purchases on my sales tax form the next time I file one and pay a 'use' tax on it. The use tax rate is the same as my state's sales tax.

Look at your sales tax return. I will bet you find a line to add in out of state purchases where no sales tax was paid at the time of purchase.

Use tax is <u>deductible</u>.

UTILITIES –
Utilities are <u>deductible</u>. Utilities can include gas, electric, heating fuel, water, sewer, and garbage pick up.

Special rules apply to home-based businesses. See the chapter on the home office deduction for more information.

Small Business Deductions – V's

Keep in mind that all business deductions must be
ordinary, necessary and reasonable.

VACATION FACILITES –
The IRS has restrictions on vacation facilities, especially
when made available to employees. The Tax Courts,
however, have ruled that vacation facilities for employees
are fully <u>deductible</u>.

If you own or lease a vacation facility, be sure to talk to
your tax professional. I am sure they will want to go
check it out in person to make sure it meets all of the
IRS's requirements.

VANDALISM –
Damages caused by vandalism are <u>deductible</u> to the
extent not covered by insurance.

See Theft Losses for more information on how to
calculate the loss (or gain).

VEHICLES –
All expenses for operating a business vehicle, except
commuting expenses, are <u>deductible</u>.

Please refer back to Automobile Expenses for more
information.

Small Business Deductions – W, X, Y, Z's

Keep in mind that all business deductions must be **_ordinary, necessary and reasonable._**

WAGES –
Wages you pay your employees are <u>deductible</u>.

See Payroll Expenses for more information.

WAREHOUSE –
The cost of renting a warehouse is <u>deductible</u>.

The cost of purchasing or constructing a warehouse is <u>depreciated</u>.

WEB SITE –
The cost of setting up and maintaining a web site <u>is deductible</u>, as are hosting fees.

If the cost of setting up the site is substantial and you expect to have the same basic site for several years, you may have to amortize it over three years.

The cost of Internet access is deductible if used only for business purposes. Any personal use will require pro-rating the fees and deducting only the business portion. See Internet access for more information.

WORTHLESS GOODS –
Worthless inventory is <u>deductible</u> and written off as part of Cost of Goods Sold.

If fixed assets become worthless, only the amount that has not been previously expensed (through depreciation or as an expense) can be written off.

YELLOW PAGES –
Advertising in the yellow pages is <u>deductible</u>.

ZONING –
Cost of zoning permits, filing, hearings, appeals, petitions and the like <u>are deductible</u>.

Employee versus Independent Contractor

The determination of whether an individual is or is not an employee is based on all the facts and circumstances. The IRS uses a 20-factor test in determining whether an individual is an employee or independent contractor. The 20 factors are:

INSTRUCTIONS:
An individual who must comply with instructions about when, where, and how to work is usually an employee.

TRAINING:
An employee is usually trained to perform services in a particular manner; independent contractors ordinarily use their own methods and receive no training from the person for whom they are working.

INTEGRATION:
An employee's services are usually integrated into the business operations because the services are important to the success of the business.

SERVICES RENDERED PERSONALLY:
An employee renders services personally. This shows that the employer is interested in the methods as well as the results. Independent contractors may or may not provide services personally.

HIRING ASSISTANTS:
An employee works for an employer who hires, supervises, and pays others to assist him. An independent contractor can hire, supervise, and pay assistants independently.

CONTINUING RELATIONSHIP:
An employee generally has a continuing relationship with an employer. A continuing relationship may exist even if work is performed at recurring although irregular intervals. Independent contractors generally complete the job they were hired for and do not provide on-going services.

SET WORKING HOURS:
An employee usually has set hours of work established by the employer. An independent contractor sets his or her own work hours within the scope of the job they are hired to do.

FULL-TIME EMPLOYMENT:
An employee may be required to work full-time. This indicates control by the employer. An independent contractor can work when and for whom he chooses.

WORK DONE ON PREMISES:
An employee usually works at the employer's premises or at a location designated by the employer.

ORDER OR SEQUENCE SET:
An employee may be required to perform services in the order or sequence set by the employer. Independent contractors can often chose when and in what order they will complete the job.

REPORTS:
A requirement that a worker submits regular reports indicates a degree of control.

PAYMENTS:
An employee is generally paid hourly, weekly, or monthly. An independent contractor is usually paid by the job or contract or on a straight commission.

EXPENSES:
An employee's business and travel expenses are generally paid by his employer. Unless otherwise contractually arranged, an independent contractor is responsible for his own expenses in connection with a contract or job.

TOOLS AND MATERIALS:
An employee is normally furnished tools, materials, and other equipment by the employer. Independent contractors usually provide their own tools and equipment.

INVESTMENT:
Investment in the facilities used by an independent contractor indicates that he is not an employee.

PROFIT OR LOSS:
An independent contractor can make a profit or suffer a loss.

WORKS FOR MORE THAN ONE PERSON OR FIRM:
An independent contractor is generally free to provide his services to two or more unrelated persons or firms at the same time.

OFFERS SERVICES TO THE GENERAL PUBLIC:
An independent contractor makes his services available to the general public on a regular and consistent basis.

RIGHT TO FIRE:
An employee can be fired by his employer. An independent contractor cannot be fired so long as he produces a result that meets the specifications of the contract.

RIGHT TO QUIT:

An employee can quit his job at any time without incurring liability. An independent contractor usually agrees to complete a specific job and is responsible for its satisfactory completion or is legally obligated to make good for failure to complete it.

TIP: An employer can get a ruling on whether an individual is an employee by filing Form SS-8, Determination of Employee Work Status for Purposes of Federal Employment Taxes and Income Tax Withholding. The form presents the 20 factors as a series of questions and answers, relevant under the common law test. However, submitting the Form SS-8 to the IRS can raise enough questions to cause a payroll tax audit of the employer and/or an income tax audit of the employee/independent contractor.

If an employer incorrectly classifies employees as independent contractors and has no reasonable basis for doing so, the employer is liable for taxes and penalties. However, an employer may be relieved of liability if he had a reasonable basis, such as judicial precedent (court rulings), published rulings or a specific ruling from the IRS, an employment tax audit, or long-standing industry practice (everybody in the _____ business does it this way), for not treating an individual as an employee, even if the individual is an employee under common-law standards.

The relief is available if (1) the taxpayer did not treat the worker as an employee at any time during the worker's tenure with the taxpayer, and (2) for periods after December 31, 1978, all federal returns (including Forms 1099) that the taxpayer was required to file with respect to that worker for the period are filed as if the individual were a non-employee.

The second requirement is applied on a period-by-period basis; thus, failing to file Form 1099 for a worker for one particular year will not necessarily disqualify an employer from relief for that worker for a subsequent year.

Remember, with the IRS, it is definitely better to ask permission than forgiveness. They don't have much of a sense of humor over there.

The Truth About the Home Office Deduction

The Best Thing Since Sliced Bread – Or Not?

There are many people out there, tax professionals and otherwise, who are promoting the Home Office Deduction as the best thing since sliced bread for the home-based business owner, but is it really?

There are specific rules relating to the home office deduction; rules on who can take the deduction and who can't. Rules on what and how much can be deducted and when. These rules apply to individuals, trusts, estates, partnerships and S corporations. The only type of entity they do not apply to are C corporations. Not everyone who runs a business out of their home will qualify for the deduction.

The purpose of this chapter is to give you, the taxpayer, an understanding of the rules that apply so you can make an informed decision on whether or not you qualify for this deduction and whether or not you want to take it if you do qualify. Keep in mind that you may qualify to take the deduction, but the actual amount you get to deduct may be limited.

The term home includes a house, apartment, condo, mobile home or boat. It also includes structures on the property such as an unattached garage, studio, barn or greenhouse. You do not have to own the property to qualify for the deduction.

Part I – Qualifying for the Deduction

To qualify to claim expenses for business use of your home, you must meet **all** of the following tests:

169

1) Your use of the business part of your home must be:

a) **Exclusive** – you cannot use that part of your home for anything but business. If you have a den with a desk and a computer, but the rest of the family also uses it to watch TV or play games, you do not qualify. The business area does not have to be a separate room; it only has to be a separately identifiable are. There does not even have to be a permanent partition in place, but you do have to be able to separate your business area from your personal area.

The only exclusions to this test are the parts of you home used to store inventory or product samples or if you run a day-care facility. If you use part of your basement to store inventory that part would qualify for the home office deduction even if you use the rest of the basement for personal purposes.

To qualify for deduction based on the storage of inventory:

- your business must involve the sale of products at wholesale or retail,
- your home must be the only fixed location of your business,
- the storage use must be regular **and**
- it must be a separately identifiable space.

b) **Regular** – the business use of this area of your home must be on a continuing basis though it does not have to be every day.

c) **For your trade or business** – the use has to relate to the carrying on of your business.

Investment activities, such as reading and research, that are not your trade or business do not qualify.

2) In addition, the business part of your home must meet **one** of the following requirements:

a) It must be your principal place of business. We will look at this requirement in a minute.

b) A place where you meet or deal with patients, clients or customers in the normal course of your trade or business.

c) A separate structure (not attached to your home) you use in connection with your trade or business.

For example, I have a small cabin on my property that I use as the office for my accounting practice. Since I also meet clients there on a regular basis and don't use it for anything else, this qualifies me for the home office deduction.

Employees may also qualify for the home office deduction. There are a couple of additional requirements for employees. You still have to meet all of the requirements above, plus:

Your business use must be for the convenience of you employer (this depends on the facts and circumstances but does not qualify if it is merely appropriate and helpful), **and**

You do not rent any part of your home to your employer and use the rented portion to perform services as an employee.

Principal Place of Business

You can have more than one business location, including your home, for the same business. Determining your principal place of business depends on factors such as the relative importance of the activities performed at each location and the time spent at each location. To qualify for the home office deduction, your home must be your principal place of business. Your principal place of business is your home if:

1) You use it exclusively and regularly for administrative or management activities of your business, **and**

2) You have no other fixed location where you conduct substantial administrative or management activities for your business.

Some examples of administrative or management activities are billing customers or clients, keeping your books and records, ordering supplies and materials, setting appointments or writing reports. Of course there are many more duties that would qualify as administrative or managerial activities based upon your type of business but this list gives you a general idea.

Performing administrative or managerial duties at other locations does not automatically disqualify you from the home office deduction. The following activities will not disqualify your home office from being your principal place of business:

1) You have others conduct your administrative or management activities at locations other than your home. For example, an accountant that keeps your books and financial records at their office.

2) You conduct administrative or management activities at places that are not fixed locations of your business, such as a car or hotel room.
3) You occasionally conduct minimal administrative or management activities at a fixed location outside your home.
4) You conduct substantial non-administrative or non-management business activities outside your home. For example, you meet with or provide services to customers or clients at a fixed location of the business outside your home.
5) You have suitable space to conduct administrative or management activities outside your home, but choose to use your home for those activities instead.

WARNING:

If you have more than one trade or business, your principal place of business must be determined separately for each trade or business activity. One home office may be the principal place of business for more than one activity. However, you will not meet the exclusive use test for any activity unless **each** activity conducted in that office meets **all** the tests for the business use of the home deduction.

For example, you are employed as a business executive. Your principal place of business, as explained earlier, is your employer's offices. You also have a business as a representative for an MLM company. All of the work associated with the MLM company is done in your home office and the office is used exclusively for that business. If you meet all of the other tests, you can deduct expenses for the business use of your home for the MLM business.

But, let's say that you also use your home office for work related to your business executive job. In that case, you would not meet the exclusive use test for the MLM business. As an employee, you must meet the convenience of the employer test to qualify for the deduction.   You do not meet this test for your work as an executive, so you cannot claim a deduction for the business use of your home for either activity.

Place to Meet Clients or Customers

If you meet or deal with clients or customers in your home in the normal course of your business, even though you also carry on business at another location, you can deduct your expenses for the part of your home used exclusively and regularly for business if you meet the following tests:

1) You physically meet with patients, clients, or customers on your premises, and
2) Their use of your home is substantial and integral to conducting your business.

Doctors, dentists, attorneys, and other professionals who maintain offices in their homes generally will meet this requirement. Using your home for occasional meetings and telephone calls will not qualify you to deduct expenses for the business use of your home.

The part of your home, in this case, that you use exclusively and regularly to meet clients or customers does not have to be your principal place of business.

Separate Structure

You can deduct expenses for a separate free-standing structure such as a studio, garage, or barn, if you use it exclusively and regularly for your business. The structure does not have to be your principal place of business or a place where you meet clients or customers.

Part II – Taking the Deduction

Now you know if you qualify to take the home office deduction or not. Next we will look at how the deduction is calculated.

The first thing you need to do is calculate the percentage of your home that is used for business. To find the business percentage, compare the size of the part of your home that you use for business to the size of your whole house. Next you will apply that percentage to the cost of operating your home to find the business part of the expenses.

You can use any reasonable method to figure the business percentage. The most common methods are:

1. Divide the area used for business (length times width) by the total area of your home. For example, your home office is 200 square feet and your home is 2000 square feet. Your business percentage is then 10% (200 divided by 2000 times 100). This is the method most favored by the IRS.

2. If the rooms in your home are all about the same size, you can divide the number of rooms used for the business by the total number of rooms in your house. So, if your house has 4 rooms, all about the same size

and you use one for business, your business percentage is 25% (1 divided by 4 times 100).

NOTE: If you only used your home for business purposes part of the year, you can only use expenses for that time that it was used for business. Huh? Let's say you started your business on October 1st. You can only use the expenses incurred in operating your home for October, November and December, not the rest of the year, to figure your allowable deduction.

Deduction Limit

The amount of your home office deduction can be limited by the income of your business. We will look at examples following this discussion.

The next step in the home office deduction process is to calculate your business income as if you ran it from anywhere, home or office. This means you take your gross sales and deduct all of the items that would be deductible regardless of where your business is located. See our Small Business Deduction Checklist for a listing of deductible business expenses.

Basically you fill out your Schedule C down to line 29, Tentative Profit (Loss). If this amount is a loss, the only deductions you can take, in the current year, for your home office are for those items that would be deductible elsewhere on your return. These would include home mortgage interest, real estate taxes and casualty and theft losses that can be taken as itemized deductions on Schedule A of your Form 1040.

These are also the only expenses you can take (home mortgage interest, real estate taxes and casualty losses) to create a loss by the use of the home office deduction.

For example, on line 29 of Schedule C, you have calculated a tentative profit of $400. The business portion of your interest, taxes and casualty losses total $500. At this point you have a $100 loss on your Schedule C and you cannot take a deduction for the business portion of the other expenses of operating your home such as utilities, insurance, repairs and maintenance.

You can carryover the unused operating expenses and depreciation for this year to next year and take it then, if your business has enough tentative profit next year.

NOTE: If part of the gross income from your trade or business is from the business use of your home and part is from a place other than your home, you must determine the part of your gross income from the business use of your home before you figure the deduction limit. Consider the time spent at each location, the business investment in each location and any other relevant facts when making this determination.

Deducting Expenses

How much you can deduct and which expenses are deductible depends on whether the expenses you incur are direct, indirect or unrelated expenses.

Direct Expenses are those related only to the business part of your home and are fully deductible (subject to the income limitation, of course). An example would be painting your home office.

Indirect Expenses are the costs required in maintaining and running your entire home. Indirect expenses are only deductible for the business portion of your home. The business percentage calculated above is applied to these costs to calculate the amount deductible for your home office. Examples here would include insurance, utilities and general repairs affecting the whole residence.

Unrelated Expenses are those for areas of your home not used for your business and are not deductible. These would include any lawn care and repairs on a part of your home that is not your home office, such as painting your bedroom.

Some expenses are deductible whether you use your home for business or not. These expenses include real estate taxes, home mortgage interest and casualty losses. These items can be deducted on Schedule A, Itemized Deductions, regardless of the use of your home for business. If you qualify to claim business use of your home expenses, you can use the business percentage of these expenses to figure your home office deduction.

Now, some people would say, "If I can deduct them on Schedule A anyway, why would I want to fool with all of this to deduct them as a home office expense?" The biggest answer here is 15.3% self-employment taxes. Your business profit is subject to self-employment tax, your other income, generally, is not. So by converting your itemized deductions to business deductions, you reduce your self-employment tax by 15.3% (13.3% for 2011 and the first 60 days of 2012) of the amount you were able to deduct as a business expense.

NOTE: You can include the interest on a second mortgage in your calculations of deductible home mortgage interest. Home mortgage interest, itself, has limits. Generally you can only deduct (in total) the home mortgage interest on the first $1,000,000 of indebtedness or the first $100,000 of a home equity loan. Consult a tax professional if your home mortgage debt exceeds these limits.

Casualty losses on the home you use for your business must be directly related expenses to be fully deductible as a home office expense or indirectly related expenses to be partially deductible as a home office expense.

Insurance can be deducted for the portion covering the business part of your home. You need to look at your insurance policy though. If your policy covers more than one year, you can only deduct the amount that covers the current year. So, if your policy covers April 1 through March 31, you have to use 3 months of last year's premium and 9 months of this year's premium.

Rent paid on your home can be deducted by applying your business percentage to the total rent payments for the year. If you own your home, you cannot deduct the fair rental value of your home; you can only use the actual expenses of purchasing and maintaining your home.

Repairs and maintenance costs can be deducted for the business portion of your home. This includes labor costs other than your own labor (which is non-deductible). Repairs and maintenance can be direct costs or indirect costs and should be treated appropriately.

Security systems protecting your entire home can be classified as an indirect expense. Generally, there are two parts to a security system, the system itself and the monthly monitoring fees. You can deduct the monthly fees by applying your business percentage to the total fees. The cost of the system itself, generally, must be depreciated (written off over several years). You can take a deduction for the business percentage of the depreciation allowed.

The costs for **utilities and other services**, which are normally non-deductible, can be taken as a home office expense by applying your business percentage to the total cost. Examples would include electricity, gas, water, trash removal and cleaning expenses. Lawn care and maintenance costs are NOT deductible.

The cost of the first **telephone** line into your house in non-deductible, including taxes. The IRS figures you are going to have a telephone, whether you have a business in your home or not. Any long-distance charges on that phone that relate to your business, though, are fully deductible on your business return, regardless of whether or not you qualify for the home office deduction. Likewise, if you have a second line in your home used exclusively for business, you can deduct the entire cost on your business return.

Depreciation is the method used to write off an asset (something you own) over a period of years. Rather than take an expense in the year that you bought it, the cost is spread out over time. The thought behind this is that the item (like your house, office equipment, office furniture, etc.) will benefit more than one year, so should be expensed in more than one year.

Depreciation is complex and really beyond the scope of this report, but I will try to give you some general information to help you calculate your home depreciation for the home office deduction. Keep in mind that you cannot depreciate land, only the house that stands on the land. Think of it this way, if the house was gone, the land would still be worth something. So you must separate the value of the land from the value of your house.

First you calculate the adjusted basis of your house. For most people this would be the amount they paid for it (excluding the cost of the land) plus the cost of any major improvements (like a new roof) or renovations minus any depreciation or casualty losses taken in prior years.

Next you calculate the fair market value of your home (excluding the cost of the land). Fair market value is the price at which the property would change hands between a willing seller and a willing and able buyer. You may want to consult a real estate agent or appraiser for the sales of similar properties in the same area on or about the date you begin using your home for business.

Once you have these two numbers calculated, you will use the lesser of the two to calculate your depreciation deduction. A home office is considered non-residential real property for the purposes of depreciation and, as such, will be expensed (or depreciated) over 39 years beginning in the middle of the month you began using it for business. The IRS has tables listing the percentages for each year and month, but basically it works like this (using Adjusted Basis): Adj. Basis divided by 468 (39 years x 12 months) times the number of months left in the year plus one-half.

So if the adjusted basis of your home was $100,000 (excluding land) and you began your home-based business in March, your depreciation would be $2030 (rounded to the next dollar). $100,000 / 468 x 9.5 = $2030. You would then apply your business percentage to this number. If you used 20% of your home for business purposes, the amount of depreciation you could deduct for the home office deduction would be $2030 x 20% or $406.

Sale or Exchange of Your Home

Current tax law allows you to exclude up to $250,000 ($500,000 for married, filing joint) of the gain on the sale of your home if you meet certain ownership and use tests. Basically, if you have owned the home for at least two years and have lived in the home as your main home for at least two years, you qualify for the exclusion. Remember this exclusion is on the gain (sales price less adjusted basis) not on the sales price, so it has potentially huge tax consequences.

If you used part of the home for business during the ownership and use periods, the exclusion generally only applies to the personal part of your home. If you were entitled to take depreciation on your home, because it was used for business during this time, you cannot exclude the part of your gain equal to any depreciation for periods after May 6, 1997.

What this means to you is that when you sell your house, you have to divide the sale into two parts, the personal part and the business part. Likewise, you would have to divide the adjusted basis of your house into two corresponding parts, personal and business. The amount of the gain on the business part is subject to what we call depreciation recapture. Basically, you have to pay tax on the gain of the business portion, which in most cases, is equal to the amount of depreciation you have taken in previous years.

NOTE: You must adjust the amount of your basis by the depreciation you **could have** taken, whether you took it or not. Some people say, "Well I just won't take the depreciation". It doesn't work that way. If you were entitled to take depreciation and didn't, you still have to act as if you did when you sell your property.

Examples:

John Taxpayer began his home-based business in March. He qualifies to take the home office deduction. The lower of the adjusted basis or fair market value of his home is $100,000 and he uses 20% of his home for business. From March through December he paid the following expenses:

Home mortgage interest:	$4,500
Real estate taxes:	$ 800
Utilities	$1,000
Insurance	$ 700
Office Painting	$ 500
Home Furnace Repair	$1,200

Example 1:

John had gross sales of $50,000 and deductible business expenses (before the home office deduction) of $30,000. This gives him a tentative profit of $20,000.

John's home office deduction is $2,546, calculated as follows:

Tentative Profit:	$20,000
Less 20% of Interest and	
Taxes $5,300 x .20	$ 1,060
	$18,940

Less 20% of Insurance, Utilities and
Indirect Repairs $2,800 x .20 $ 580
Less 100% of Direct Repairs $ 500
                                                      $17,880
Less Depreciation (see example above) $ 406
                                                      $17,474

Home Office Deduction = $1,060 + $580 + $500 + $406
= $2,546

John saved about $360 in self-employment taxes and
$178 in regular income tax. Remember that his home
mortgage interest and real estate taxes would have been
deductible on his Schedule A if he had not qualified for
the home office deduction.

In this scenario, John is entitled to take his full home
office deduction because he had enough tentative profit
to absorb all of the expenses. But, what if he didn't have
enough profit?

Example 2:

John had gross sales of $10,000 and deductible business
expenses of $9,000, giving him a tentative profit of
$1,000.

In this case John's home office deduction is $1,060, the
amount equal to the business portion of his home
mortgage interest and real estate taxes.

Tentative Profit: $1,000

Less 20% of Interest and

Taxes $5,300 x .20 $1,060
                                                      ($60)

Less 20% of Insurance, Utilities and Indirect Repairs $2,800 x .20	$ 580
Less 100% of Direct Repairs	$ 500
	-0-
Less Depreciation (see example above)	$ 406
	-0-

The $1,080 in operating expenses and $406 of depreciation will be carried forward to the next year and can be deducted then, provided John has enough profit to absorb this year's and next year's expenses.

His Schedule C (Form 1040) will show a $60 loss that can be used to offset other income he may have. John will have saved about $140 in self-employment tax.

Conclusions

Where does all of this leave us? To take the deduction or not take the deduction, that is the question. Every person's tax situation is unique. We can look at one item of tax law, such as the home office deduction, but every aspect of your tax return must be weighed in your final decision.

There are a couple of situations where you probably would not want to take the deduction:

1. If you are in a loss situation before the deduction, you may not want to take the home office deduction. Remember that, in this situation, you are only allowed home mortgage interest, real estate taxes and casualty losses. These items can be deducted as Itemized Deductions on Schedule A anyway, so you will not lose them if you have other income to offset them against. And you have no self-employment income to be subject to the 15.3% self-employment tax.

2. If you will only be in your house for a short period of time and are in an appreciating housing market. Remember that you can exclude up to $250,000 ($500,000 for married filing joint) of gain on the sale of your residence. If you have been eligible to claim depreciation, whether you claimed it or not, you cannot exclude the gain on the amount of depreciation. This is taxed as recaptured depreciation at 25%. You will have to split the sale of your house into the personal aspect and the business aspect.

3. The business percentage use of your home is very small, say 10% or less, you may not want to take the deduction. The benefit you gain may not be worth the time and effort to calculate the deduction.

4. Your fear of being audited. The home office deduction remains one of the IRS's most scrutinized deductions. Not that I suggest you don't take it if you qualify just because you are afraid of being audited. If you are entitled to it and it benefits your overall tax situation, take it, by all means. Just make sure that your records are in great shape and you can prove all deductions. Not only as relates to the home office deduction, but for your entire tax return.

The final answer is the one most common when discussing general tax questions: it depends.
It depends on all aspects of your tax situation, past, present and future. When in doubt, consult a competent tax professional who is familiar with your tax situation.

Where Do You Go From Here?

That concludes our discussion on income taxes for the small and/or home based business owner. I thank you very much for your purchase and hope it provided you with answers to your tax questions and/or a point to begin discussion with your own tax professional.

If there is something else you would like to see in this e-book, if there is something you read here that is not clear or you have further questions or would like to make a comment, please feel free to click here to send me an e-mail:
info@mytaxtutor.com

I also offer tax (saving) planning services. If you would like me and my staff to work on a comprehensive tax savings plan for you and your business, please send me an e-mail or call my office at the number listed below. I will tell you up front if I can provide you with tax saving strategies, before you pay me a dime. This would not take the place of your tax professional, but rather would be an outline of what types of tax savings strategies that you can work on with your tax professional to implement.

Sincerely,

Joni M. Becker, CPA
D. C. Schluter, Ltd.
1225 Highway 60 West
Faribault, MN 55021

www.ingramcontent.com/pod-product-compliance
Lightning Source LLC
Chambersburg PA
CBHW051502170526
45166CB00001B/356